THE BEGINNING
OF MARKETING THOUGHT
IN THE UNITED STATES
and
FIFTY YEARS OF MARKETING
IN RETROSPECT

*This is a volume in the
Arno Press collection*

A CENTURY OF MARKETING

Advisory Editor
Henry Assael

Associate Editor
Larry J. Rosenberg

Editorial Board
Robert Bartels
Ewald T. Grether
Stanley C. Hollander
William Lazer

*See last pages of this volume
for a complete list of titles.*

THE BEGINNING OF MARKETING THOUGHT IN THE UNITED STATES
and
FIFTY YEARS OF MARKETING IN RETROSPECT

Paul D. Converse

ARNO PRESS
A New York Times Company
New York • 1978

ST. PHILIPS COLLEGE LIBRARY

658.8
C 766b

Editorial Supervision: JOSEPH CELLINI

Reprint Edition 1978 by Arno Press Inc.

The Beginning of Marketing Thought in the United States has been reprinted from a copy in the Pennsylvania State Library.

A CENTURY OF MARKETING
ISBN for complete set: 0-405-11156-8
See last pages of this volume for titles.

Manufactured in the United States of America

Library of Congress Cataloging in Publication Data

Converse, Paul Dulaney, 1889-
 The beginning of marketing thought in the United States and Fifty years of marketing in retrospect.

 (A Century of marketing)
 Reprint of the author's 2 works, published in 1959 by the Bureau of Business Research, University of Texas, Austin, which were issued as its Studies in marketing no. 3 and no. 5 respectively.

 Bibliography: p.
 1. Marketing--United States. I. Converse, Paul Dulaney, 1889- Fifty years of marketing in retrospect. 1978. II. Title: The beginning of marketing thought in the United States. III. Series. IV. Series: Texas. University. Bureau of Business Research. Studies in marketing ; no. 3, [etc.]
HF5415.1.C59 1978 658.8 78-282
ISBN 0-405-11161-4

STUDIES IN MARKETING NO. 3

The Beginning of Marketing Thought in the United States

With Reminiscences of Some of the Pioneer Marketing Scholars

Paul D. Converse
Visiting Professor of Marketing
The University of Texas

BUREAU OF BUSINESS RESEARCH
THE UNIVERSITY OF TEXAS
Austin
1959

Foreword

Paul D. Converse has long been associated with marketing in the United States. During his many years of tenure as professor of business at the University of Illinois, he developed a national reputation as an authority in the field. In this bulletin, *The Beginning of Marketing Thought in the United States with Reminiscences of Some of the Pioneer Marketing Scholars,* Dr. Converse has made a real and unique contribution to the literature available on marketing. His personal reminiscences, because he has worked in marketing so long, are valuable to those who are teaching and working in marketing now and will be helpful to those associated with the field in the years to come. Furthermore, many will find the summary of references to be a useful aid in research.

Dr. Converse had planned originally to mimeograph the material included in this bulletin for use by his students in graduate classes at The University of Texas while he was visiting professor of marketing during the spring semester of the 1958–59 school year. However, since much of the data included was of general interest to those associated with marketing and since some of the material was not available in printed form elsewhere, the staff of the Bureau of Business Research asked his permission to publish the manuscript and make it available for sale as the third number in its Studies in Marketing series.

Elizabeth R. Turpin edited the bulletin. Dr. A. H. Chute, professor of retailing, and Dr. E. W. Cundiff, professor of marketing, both members of the faculty of the College of Business Administration, The University of Texas, made a number of suggestions which were particularly helpful to the editor. Members of the Bureau of Business Research staff who assisted Mrs. Turpin with various phases of copy preparation were: Florence Escott, Arvid Anderson, Merle Danz, Roberta Steele, Robert Dorsett, and Danny P. Rosas.

STANLEY A. ARBINGAST
Assistant Director
Bureau of Business Research

February 1, 1959

Table of Contents

	Page
Preface	vii

Chapter
- I. SOME MARKETING THOUGHT PRIOR TO 1900 . . 1
    - Edward Atkinson 3
    - David A. Wells 5
    - Arthur B. Farquhar, Henry Farquhar 7
    - Henry C. Emery 9
    - Harlow Gale 10
- II. DEVELOPMENTS IN MARKETING, 1900–1939 . . 13
    - 1900–1919 13
    - The 1920's 14
    - The 1930's 17
- III. THE PIONEER SCHOLARS 20
    - Beginnings 20
    - Writers and Researchers, 1900–1916 25
        - Walter Dill Scott 25
        - Earnest Elmo Calkins 30
        - S. Roland Hall 32
        - Ralph Starr Butler 32
        - J. George Frederick 34
        - Charles Coolidge Parlin 36
        - Arch W. Shaw 38
        - Paul T. Cherington 43
        - L. D. H. Weld 45
        - Wheeler Sammons 49
        - Paul Nystrom 50

    Scholars, 1917–1923 55
        W. H. S. Stevens 55
        Archer Wall Douglas 58
        C. S. Duncan 60
        Melvin T. Copeland 61
        Horace Secrist 63
        Fred E. Clark 65
        Frederick A. Russell 67
        W. D. Moriarty 68
        Daniel Starch 71

IV. CONTRIBUTIONS, 1925–1939 74
    Notable Studies 75

SUMMARY OF REFERENCES 79

Preface

While people have thought about the process of marketing ever since barter began among primitive people, the term "marketing thought" is used here to denote the written thought about marketing as a separate part or concept of business or the economic system.

Marketing was recognized as a separate subject about 1900, and although the first books dealing with the field of marketing did not appear until after this time, several earlier books dealt with some aspects of marketing. The first college courses in the subject were offered as early as 1902, but obviously these courses were quite different from present-day courses.

There are two main reasons for preparing this manuscript. First, the younger men in the marketing field should know, and want to know, something of the men who made the early studies, and who wrote the first books, articles, and pamphlets. However, since information about these men is not readily available, advanced students and the younger men in teaching and research (*i.e.*, men under forty-five years of age) have not had an opportunity to know much about their professional forebears. I hope this study partially fills their need.

Second, I am told that it is desirable that a contemporary should record his knowledge about these men and their personalities. Unfortunately, perhaps, I have deleted some personal material on the advice of critics who think a study such as this should be entirely objective. I knew more than half of the men whose work is sketched during their productive years, and I became acquainted with others of the group later. I knew these men professionally—that is, I knew their work at the time it appeared, and I knew the background against which the studies were made and the books and articles written. Up to the late 1920's those of us in the marketing field were "desperate" for information, and we read and studied every publication, whether presented as fact or as theory. Much of the information presented here is subjective with the resultant advantages and disadvantages.

No one knows the limitations of this manuscript better than I. It is too early to have a sound perspective from which to judge the lasting value of these early contributions. It should be borne in mind, however, that all marketing information was valuable during this period. Some readers may say that my treatment of the various pioneer writers is too short; others, that I have omitted men who should have been included; and still others, that I have included some who should have been omitted. However, since this study is limited largely to general marketing, this means that many scholars writing about the marketing of farm products, foreign trade, transportation, salesmanship, and credits and collections are not included.

Undoubtedly, later students will have the opportunity to do a much better job than I have done.

1958   PAUL D. CONVERSE

CHAPTER I

Some Marketing Thought Prior to 1900

Prior to 1900 very few writers were important in the field of marketing as such. Of the pioneers Professor Frank Coolsen,[1]* in a study of early marketing ideas and theories, discusses several empirical economists: Edward Atkinson, David A. Wells, and the Farquhars, Henry and Arthur B.[2] Two other men whose interest in marketing extended back into this early period of 1870 to 1900 are Henry C. Emery and Harlow Gale.

This period of 1870–1900 was one of agricultural and industrial expansion and of technological advances in manufacturing, mining, and agriculture (the grain binder for example). The transcontinental railroad was completed—the network of railroads was expanded in the 1870's and nearly completed in the 1880's—and the Suez Canal was opened in 1869. Iron steamships were replacing wooden sailing vessels. The telegraph was in general use and was speeding up communications, enabling, for example, American importers to buy in the Far East and thus bypass English wholesalers.

The United States was still largely an agricultural country but manufacturing was growing rapidly, with the output per man increasing and the welfare of the workers improving. Thus, "luxuries" were fast becoming "necessities" as consumers were benefited by falling prices which were brought about by lower transportation costs and labor-saving machinery. For example, it was said by

---

[1] University of Kentucky faculty (Ph.D. thesis at the University of Illinois, 1958: *Marketing Ideas of Selected Empirical Liberal Economists, 1870 to 1900*). The following information about Atkinson, Wells, and the Farquhars is abstracted from Coolsen's study.

* Footnotes are shown thus: 1. References to be found at the end of the study are shown in brackets: [1].

[2] These were businessmen rather than academic economists. Wells was academically trained and Henry Farquhar was a government statistician.

1

Edward Atkinson that the freight cost on all commodities shipped to New York by rail decreased from 36.6 percent of their value in New York in 1869 to 17.9 percent in 1883.[4]

After the panic year of 1873, "overproduction" was a chronic problem. The economists believed that mass production demanded mass distribution. To solve the overproduction problem, many people, including the men under consideration, felt that consolidations might be needed. They believed in competition; however, it was argued that even with consolidations there would be enough competition to regulate prices. This seems to be rather inconsistent, for the purpose of consolidations (or trusts) was to control prices. If they were unable to control prices, it did not seem that they could solve the problem of overproduction, for the idea of the "trusts" was to limit production sufficiently to stabilize or raise prices.

In *Recent Economic Changes* (1889), David A. Wells developed the idea that crises might be lessened by reducing wholesale and retail inventories and so lessen speculative buying and distress selling. He felt that this could be accomplished as a result of improved transportation and communication, and by more direct selling between manufacturers and retailers, with the manufacturers thus taking over tasks formerly performed by middlemen.

The main objectives of these early economists were the achievement of free trade and the maintenance of a competitive system. Much of their writing was designed to prove that free trade, or tariff for revenue only, was the best policy for America. Most of the arguments for and against the protective tariff were evolved during this period. It was argued, for example, that a tariff raised the prices to American consumers and farmers and so lessened their purchasing power for domestically produced goods. This, in turn, reduced the standard of living of the workingman and placed American producers at a disadvantage in selling their goods abroad.

Van Hise cites the advantages of competition as they were summarized in a speech by Roger A. Pryor in 1892:[150]

1. Competition between buyers raises the price of raw materials.
2. Competition between sellers reduces prices to consumers.

3. Reduction in prices increases number of consumers.
4. Increase in consumption increases production.
5. Increase in production increases employment.
6. Competition between employers raises wages.
7. Higher wages increase welfare of workers.
8. Competition between sellers improves quality.
9. Competition to sell reduces costs, quickens inventions of labor-saving machines and so stimulates the useful arts and sciences.

Edward Atkinson
(1827–1905)

Edward Atkinson was a businessman whose main interest was cotton manufacturing. He wrote continuously and voluminously from 1861 to 1905, producing more than two hundred and fifty pamphlets, hundreds of letters, and several books. From a marketing viewpoint, his most important books were *The Distribution of Products* (1885), *The Industrial Progress of the Nation* (1889), and *Taxation and Work* (1892). To Atkinson, marketing—or distribution (terms used interchangeably)—was the most important part of the economic system, for he felt that "upon the 2,500,000 people engaged in trade and transportation, depends the subsistence of our total population."[5] He pointed out that the best way of improving conditions was "by increasing the quantity of product and finding a market for the increase."[5] Then when lower prices raised the scale of living of the consumers, the market would be increased.

In the period from 1860 to 1885 the railroads had reduced the cost of physical distribution of goods in bulk by two-thirds. For example, from 1872 to 1887 the cost of transporting wheat from Chicago to New York including the cost of ocean shipment to Liverpool decreased 37 cents per bushel. In addition, machinery in the terminal markets reduced the cost of handling grain by 4 cents a bushel, and Atkinson guessed that machinery on the farms further reduced the cost of producing wheat by at least 3 cents a bushel, making a total reduction in Liverpool of 44 cents a bushel.[9]

Although Atkinson considered the various functions performed in marketing—buying, selling, storage, standardizing and grading, physical handling, packaging, financing, risk taking, gathering information—he did not use the word "functions," nor use the "functional" organization of his material. For example, he considered the processing of farm products as a part of the marketing process, or a marketing function, as did several other early writers. Their approach was to find the spread between the price to the farmer and the consumer, and they did not stop to draw the distinction between creation of "form" and other utilities. For 1880 he estimated the value of foodstuffs on the farm at $2,660 million and to the consumers at between $4,000 million and $4,500 million. The difference is between 33 and 40 percent—the cost of marketing farm products. However, in view of later studies his estimate was likely somewhat too low. For example, he speaks of the retailer as taking 35 percent of the price of a loaf of bread.[4]

Atkinson estimated for 1890 that the total volume of goods [6] at source amounted to $12.5 billion plus a half billion consumed at source; that they were sold once, twice, thrice, or more times on the way to the consumer, so that total volume of exchange amounted to $40 billion or more. Of this total, foreign trade made up 15 percent of the amount, or some $6 billion. His discussion antedated by forty-seven years the "flow of goods" chart presented by the Twentieth Century Fund in *Does Distribution Cost Too Much?* (1939).

Atkinson went on to say:

All we can do is move something; we can make nothing. The work of life is conversion of force, of which the end is to supply to each man, woman, and child with from two and one-half to five pounds of food a day; with from ten to twenty pounds of cotton or wool a year for our backs; and with a few boards for our dwelling place.[6]

This idea of movement antedated that of Arch Shaw, who said that marketing is matter in motion.[129]

Atkinson thought that the cost of distribution could be greatly reduced by large concerns operating on a cash-carry basis (like the English cooperatives) on a low margin per unit. He thought retail expenses of selling bread over the counter could be reduced to six percent.[4] This approach was certainly prophetic of the supermarket chains.

Of employed persons, Atkinson estimated that 10 percent had high purchasing power; 35.7 percent, medium; and 54.3 percent, low.[4] He felt a decline in prices from 1870 to 1897 was a "blessing and not a misfortune" as it raised real wages. He said that labor would obtain a constantly increasing share of the national product. He showed how demand varied between different income groups and said that the success of marketing depends on the lowest income group since more than fifty percent of the population is in this group.

Atkinson made market analyses for different types of goods, anticipating by some forty years the development of marketing research.

David A. Wells
(1828–1898)

David A. Wells received a liberal arts education at Williams College and advanced training at the Lawrence Scientific School at Harvard. His early writings were in the fields of chemistry, geology, and agriculture. He was chairman of the United States Revenue Commission from 1865 to 1870, and later chairman of the New York State Tax Commission. He was active also in organizing railroads and was a member of the Board of Arbitration of the Associated Railways. Wells was at first a protagonist of protective tariffs but he soon switched to the advocacy of free trade or tariffs for revenue only.

Of interest to marketing students were his *Practical Economics* (1885) and his *Recent Economic Changes* (1889).

Wells said that between 1870 and 1890 prices fell and the standard of living increased, resulting especially from market improvement. The purchasing power of the American workingman increased by more than one-fourth between 1860 and 1885. As Wells put it, he was "getting a steadily increasing share of the product."[155] The improvement in nutrition resulted in larger sizes and widths of clothing, and an increased demand was noted for modern housing conveniences. The long-run trend was for real wages to increase, and, through marketing processes, consumer income and demand were expanded. Wells felt that marketing makes the economy dynamic, puts the product of technical progress into the hands of the consumers, and contributes substantially to the progress of civilization. Wells was influenced by Ralph Waldo Emerson's essay, "Works and Days" (1870), in which he said the greatest "meliorator of the world is selfish huckstering trade."[41]

Three forces will continue to expand consumer demand, according to Wells: (1) reduced prices, (2) increased purchasing power of the mass market, and (3) progressive wants or changes in culture.[155]

Wells made some consumer market analyses and estimated the per capita consumption for various food products, luxuries (*e.g.*, tobacco, coffee, tea, liquor), clothing, and house maintenance. He noted that the demand for wheat does not expand indefinitely as people have higher incomes. In contrast, the demand decreases with the ability of a higher income group to procure a greater variety of food. "A man who has been contented with one shirt a week is not likely to buy seven even if he can buy seven for the price he formerly paid for one."[3]

Wells said also that as income increases, consumers (1) disdain to economize, and (2) progressively develop tastes for better things. In spite of improved living standards, both industrial and agrarian labor loudly proclaimed its discontent. Wells thought that this paradox was partly explained by the increase in intelligence or general information on the part of the masses.

The wonderful material progress which has been made within the past quarter of a century has probably done more to overcome the inertia and quicken the energy of the masses than has been hereto

[3] "The culture of the manual laborers of the world has not advanced concurrently, (immediately) in recent years, with the increased and cheapened production of such articles. Many things consequently have been showered upon these classes which they do not know how to use, and do not feel they need, and for which, therefore, they can create no market" (David A. Wells, *Recent Economic Changes* [New York: D. Appleton & Co., 1889]). However, this quote is not entirely consistent with statements later in the book.

achieved in this direction in all preceding centuries. . . . They [the masses] have come to know more of what others are doing; know better what they themselves are capable of doing; and their wants have correspondingly increased, and not merely in respect to quantities of the things to which they have always been accustomed, but very many articles and services which within a comparatively recent period were regarded as luxuries, are now almost universally considered and demanded as necessities.[155]

Wells was getting close to saying that marketing activities increase demand (income) by making people work harder or more intelligently to secure the purchasing power with which to buy the things they desire, an idea expressed by Moriarty in 1923.[4]

Wells said further that as mass income and the level of consumption increase, the buying preferences of consumers would become more uncertain and more unpredictable. This point of view anticipated a similar statement made by William H. Lough and Martin R. Gainsbrugh in *High-Level Consumption*, published in 1935.

Wells, like others, was concerned with the "chronic overproduction" of goods and with the recurring business crises. He felt that direct marketing from producer to retailer, forward selling by wholesalers, drop-shipping from manufacturers to retailers, together with the new methods of transportation and communication, would make possible the reduction in size of wholesale and retail inventories and better planning of production, thus helping to avoid crises or at least to reduce their severity.

Like Atkinson, Wells believed that the cost of distribution could be reduced by large integrated companies, eliminating middlemen by direct marketing.[155]

Arthur B. Farquhar
(1838–1925)
Henry Farquhar
(1851–1925)

Arthur B. Farquhar, a manufacturer of farm implements of York, Pennsylvania, collaborated with his brother, Henry, a government

[4] See discussion of W. D. Moriarty in Chapter III.

statistician in Coast Survey and Department of Agriculture, to write *Economic and Industrial Delusions* (1891). Arthur also wrote an autobiography with Samuel Crowther, *The First Million the Hardest* (1922), part of which appeared as a series of articles by Arthur Farquhar entitled, "My Sixty-Four Years in Business" (1856–1920), which ran in *System* magazine in 1920–1921.

Arthur Farquhar over the years exported a sizable portion of his implements. This may partially explain his advocacy of free trade. He said that during the 1880's pig iron was $10 a ton and bessemer steel $14 a ton cheaper in England than in the United States, while the freight was only $3 a ton. He felt that this placed him at a distinct disadvantage, raised prices to the farmers, and lessened their buying power for other goods. Nevertheless, his export prices averaged 5 to 10 percent below his domestic prices, and it was his policy to export 25 percent of his goods.[32]

Farquhar said that to sell the increased volume of goods produced after the Civil War, more credit was extended. During the 1870's he sold through export merchants for cash. However, by 1880 he was using agents in principal foreign cities who sold on credit.

Farquhar made goods to satisfy different markets (*i.e.*, market segments), and this, he felt, gave him an advantage over English competitors who did not follow this policy. Product differences or patent protection enabled him and some of the other manufacturers to shift in part to nonprice competition. He said that "over production is only bad distribution."[46] While the panic of September 1873 closed practically all factories, Farquhar managed to cut his prices 25 percent and soon reopened his factory.

Perhaps the main contribution of the Farquhars was in their statistical measurement of prices and the elasticity of demand. Their method was later followed by H. L. Moore and Henry Schultz.[106] They found that a larger wheat or corn crop often had a lower total value than a smaller crop. The demand for wheat was found to be more elastic than the demand for corn. Thus, in 1889 the wheat crop was 18 percent larger than in 1888, but the total value was only 11 percent more.[46] Although the production of corn and wheat had doubled since 1869, the total value of corn was the same and that of wheat only 30 percent greater.

The Farquhars also related prices to supply and population. In 14 out of 20 years an increased crop of potatoes had a lower total value. For every 1 percent by which the size of the crop varied, the total value varied 0.3 percent in the opposite direction. [46, 32]

Henry C. Emery
(1872-1924)

Henry C. Emery, for many years a member of the faculty of Yale University, was the author of a study, *Speculation on the Stock and Produce Exchanges of the United States* (1896), published in the Columbia University Studies in History, Economics, and Public Law. In this work he advanced the theory that speculation on organized exchanges tended to lessen the major fluctuations in prices although increasing the number of minor fluctuations. Short-selling increases supply when prices rise, and he felt it limits the advance. Then when prices drop, the short-sellers must buy to cover their contracts, and this covering supports prices. According to Emery, "thus prices at both ends of a panic are less extreme than they would be without short selling."[43]

Emery presented figures on the fluctuations of prices of wheat, corn, and cotton before and after organized speculation was started. The figures showed that the width of fluctuations was less in the later periods. However, other factors such as improved transportation facilities (with the building of the railroads), improved storage facilities, and more market information may have been responsible. For these and other reasons, "statistics can hardly be used to furnish either proof or disproof of the foregoing estimate of the effect of speculation."[43]

Emery's theory was widely used for several years in teaching economics and marketing. Some twenty years later, W. H. S. Stevens, in his study of grain marketing for the Federal Trade Commission, made a large statistical study but was unable to either prove or disprove the theory that speculation on organized exchanges tended to stabilize prices. Whether or not the Federal Trade Commission study was responsible, much less attention has been given to this theory in recent years.

In addition to this study on speculation, Emery published a manual (in London) called *Company Management*,[42] and numerous pamphlets that made available his lectures on a variety of subjects.

Harlow Gale
(1862–1945)

Harlow Gale, who taught psychology at the University of Minnesota, was a real pioneer whose influence on other men in the marketing field, such as Walter Dill Scott, will be shown in their sketches.

In 1895 Gale sent questionnaires to 200 business firms, mostly in Minneapolis-St. Paul, asking them their opinions of advertising, the aim of their advertising, and the most effective ways to induce people to buy. He also interviewed a number of large advertisers.

As early as 1896–97 he used his students in controlled experiments to measure the attention value of advertising. These experiments were continued for a number of years and perhaps mark the modern beginning of the application of the scientific method in the study of marketing. One of his students, Horace C. Klein, described the experiments which the class undertook, and pointed out that from these data they were able to prove that a right-hand page was always seen before a left-hand page and that the back cover was much more valuable than any inside page.[5]

---

[5] "We spent Saturday afternoons for a year in a dark room on the top floor of the old Main Building. With the use of lantern slides, etc., the members of the class made thousands of experiments to find, for example, what combinations of colors attract the eye.

"We built a little machine which would turn the pages of a magazine rapidly. With this we made something like 200,000 tests, using all the members of our class in rotation, and spent two or three hours every Saturday afternoon in a dark room turning the pages of the magazines with a flash light shining on the pages. Each observer wrote down what he saw. We then compiled the figures, and proved that a right-hand page was always seen before a left-hand page. We also proved that the back cover was very much

After graduation, Klein went to work for an advertising agency. On one occasion, finding that what he considered a choice location for his ads failed to get the expected results, he started making notes on the way people read magazines and found that most women and young people opened the magazine at the first page while most men began looking at the advertising pages in the back. Since his product appealed primarily to men he had his ads placed on the outer column nearest the back cover and found that

the cost of an inquiry dropped one half . . . but I never would have found out the facts had it not been for the experiments we made under Professor Gale and his frequently cautioning us to be sure that we had considered all the variables in connection with any conclusion we might draw.[158]

Gale wrote an article *"On the Psychology of Advertising,"* published in *Psychological Studies* in July 1900, which reports the results of some of his experiments.

In this study, he broke ads down into relevant words and cuts, and into irrelevant words and cuts. Some of his conclusions can be noted as follows: Attention was best gained by relevant words or text, next by relevant and irrelevant cuts, and least of all by irrelevant words; through five repetitions the relevant words increased steadily in value while the cuts decreased, and irrelevant words remained on their initially low level; females were attracted more than males by cuts and by irrelevancy; males were attracted mostly by black and green, and females mostly by red and green; there was a progressive increase of attention within the sizes of type from 2 to 5 mm high; the left side of the page was seen more than the right; the horizontal quarter above the middle was on the whole more effective than the other quarters, with the bottom decidedly the least valuable.

---

more valuable than any inside page. Again, my figures may be wrong but I have quoted them for fifty years so believe that they are right.

"It is easy to appreciate the fact that our work in a dark room in an attic, in a very old building, in the warm weather, (in early fall and late spring), and especially on Saturday afternoons, might have been a little tedious for boys and girls in their Senior year" (Letter of June 21, 1954, from Horace C. Klein).

Gale also studied the effectiveness of advertising and said:

Only about half of our informants [students] seemed to be influenced consciously by advertising; the females somewhat more than the males. But a considerable amount of advertising acts upon people below the threshold of their conscious attention and memories.[65]

Walter Dill Scott acknowledged his indebtedness to Gale when he started work at Northwestern University. Chicago had an advertising club which encouraged Scott to write and paid him for his articles. On the other hand, Minneapolis-St. Paul had no such club and Gale received no such encouragement. Perhaps if he had, there would be more of a written record of his work. Unfortunately, he seems to have left only a couple of pamphlets in addition to the article from which the above conclusions are quoted. However, Gale influenced Scott and Scott influenced Starch, as is shown later under the sketches of these men.

CHAPTER II

Developments in Marketing, 1900–1939

1900–1919

When the century opened, the country was recovering from the long and severe depression of the 1890's. Recovery was the result of several factors including gold from the Klondyke, the Spanish-American War, demand for farm products in western Europe, and the low price of steel initiated by Andrew Carnegie—the lowest price of steel in the history of the world.

Wholesalers were well established, some of whom already had their own brands. Local wholesalers were being established in the smaller cities and towns, and traveling salesmen (drummers and specialty men) were in their heyday. Chain stores, especially variety and grocery chains in the East, were becoming important, and the mail-order houses were growing rapidly. The business barons—Carnegie, Rockefeller, Frick, Vanderbilt, Morgan, Gould, Hill, and others—were still "in the saddle." The first few years of this period were characterized by the "trust movement"—the consolidation and mergers of small companies into larger ones.

The economy expanded rapidly between 1900 and 1919, with a strong export demand for farm products. Manufacturing also expanded, especially in metal products, oil, office machines, and shoes —with American kerosene, typewriters, and shoes being exported to many parts of the world.

The important innovations of the period were automobiles and moving pictures. In the field of transportation, there was a start on improved or "good" roads. The railroad network had been completed, but large sums were expended for more and better tracks, larger locomotives, and more and larger freight cars. Many lines were double-tracked, and in some places the tracks were quadrupled. In addition, the electric interurbans were built in the early

1900's. The electric streetcar systems were expanding, and the telephone was coming into general use.

Improved cooking stoves (ranges), kitchen cabinets, running water in homes, and inside plumbing all came into more general use. There was daily delivery of ice in most towns and cities, and many families had ice refrigerators. There was a great increase in the use of electricity, and electric appliances such as washing machines, irons, vacuum cleaners came into use. R.F.D. routes were established throughout the country. Premiums and trading stamps were in wide use.

There was a great outcry against "trusts" and monopolies, and the Clayton anti-trust and the Federal Trade Commission acts were passed by Congress.

Prices were rising, and there was a great protest against the high cost of living, apparently because prices rose faster than wages and salaries. From an economic and social viewpoint, this period might well be called the "high cost of living era." Yet the standard of living was also rising, as indicated by the phrase, "the cost of high living."

The theory of prices generally taught was the "marginal" theory. The application of this during World War I as the "bulk line" theory led the Government to set very high prices for several products. The War and the postwar boom afterwards led to still higher prices, which then broke sharply in 1920.

The 1920's

Prices reached their peak during the first half of 1920, and then broke. The decline was rapid, almost fifty percent from the summer of 1920 to the spring of 1921. However, recovery was very rapid, and the economy was in full swing by the middle of 1922. This was a severe but short depression, and losses on inventories were heavy. However, the great majority of businesses had enough resources accumulated during the War and postwar boom period to carry them through.

Europe got its farms in devastated areas back into production quickly. It was extremely short of foreign exchanges, so export demand for food products declined greatly in the summer of 1920.

This caused a quick and drastic decline in the prices of many farm products and the "farm problem" developed. This was a period of "frozen assets," as prices were declining, and "hand to mouth or small-order buying" set in as is usual during periods of rapidly declining prices. A "buyers' strike" developed, meaning that the consumers were holding off for lower prices.

Recovery was quick and rapid. The consumers had many unfilled wants and still had some purchasing power in reserve. To encourage buying, many sellers adopted a policy of guaranteeing their prices against decline to both dealers and consumers. Henry Ford's action in guaranteeing the price of his cars was especially important. With confidence restored, consumer purchasing quickly responded. Prices had declined about fifty percent and the price level was almost stationary from 1922 through 1928.

The 1920's was an interesting decade. American factories had expanded during the War and had acquired more "know-how." This was especially true of the chemical industries. Before the War the United States had been dependent upon Germany for dyes. When this supply was cut off, a dye industry had to be created quickly.

Since people were buying automobiles in great numbers, there was a demand for highways on which to operate the cars. With the building of surfaced highways as one of the important developments of the decade, the 1920's became the "highway-building decade." The radio came into general use in the mid-twenties as did the electric refrigerator. The motor truck had come into local use in the 1910's, and the War had boosted its importance. Inter-city trucking began and grew rapidly in the 1920's. The movement of mail and passengers by air was begun.

From a marketing viewpoint, the 1920's might be called the "chain-store decade," for chain stores grew rapidly and spread to all parts of the country. Their appeal was due primarily to low prices, although cleanliness of stores and freshness of stock were important. There was a great deal of anti-chain propaganda. Independent retailers were hurt and waged campaigns for restrictive legislation. A start was made in voluntary group wholesaling and there was some growth among retailer-owned wholesale houses, as well as in the development of retail buying groups. Wholesalers had much to learn about operating as semi-integrated organizations, but considerable progress was made, especially in the grocery trade.

There was an increase in installment sales of consumer goods, and the soundness of installment selling was widely and heatedly debated.

The big decline in farm prices in 1920 led to the "farm problem" which has been present ever since. Aid for the farmers was primarily in extension of credit and in growth (with government help) of cooperative marketing organizations. By and large, the relation between prices received by farmers for their products and the prices paid for goods was allowed to follow natural lines, and by 1929 it appeared that the "farm problem" was disappearing. Then came the depression of the 1930's!

The popular price theory of the 1920's was stable prices. This was, perhaps, a natural reaction from the rapid decline in prices in 1920. The common opinion seems to have been that if prices were stable, buyers would not increase and decrease inventories; there would be no ups and downs in business; and the "business cycle" would disappear. Businessmen felt that they were justified in stabilizing their prices. There was a rather widespread demand that the Sherman Law be amended to permit price agreements. There was also a growing demand for resale-price maintenance laws.

The belief in stable prices is an old one. It had many advocates in the years preceding World War I, but they were in the minority. Another old theory strongly advocated by the American Federation of Labor was that high wages should be paid to increase the purchasing power of workers and to create larger sales for business.

Prices from 1922 to 1929 were relatively stable. Output per worker increased, and unemployment increased in the latter part of the decade, apparently because the consumers could not buy enough goods to keep the factories busy. Prices were steady, but a severe depression started in 1929.

The 1930's

The decade of the 1930's was one of depression. Several explanations have been offered: (1) output per worker had been increasing, (2) prices were stable in the 1920's, (3) prices did not decline, (4) consumer purchasing power did not increase sufficiently to keep labor fully employed. Another important cause was the completion of the big highway building program. It has been pointed out that depressions often follow the completion of large construction programs (such as that of 1837 following the building of the canals and that of 1893 following the completion of the network of railroads). Another factor also was the curtailment of European purchases owing to lack of dollar exchange.

The depression was long and severe. Business had accepted the theory that prices should be stable, and it was remembered that the depression of 1920 had been short. For this reason, many believed that this depression also would be short, and they expected business to pick up in late 1930 or 1931. But prices fell slowly, and, in addition, paying off installment debts contracted in the 1920's reduced consumer purchasing power somewhat.

There were several innovations but they were not of sufficient importance to bring about recovery—air-conditioning of trains, restaurants, and theaters; colored pictures; talking moving pictures; diesel locomotives; paper milk bottles; refrigerated locker plants; quick-frozen foods; dry ice; plastics; steel houses; and others are examples. None of these, however, developed a really important industry. There was an increase in the electrical power produced, rural electrification, air travel, intercity trucking, and appliances for the home.

Out of this depression grew a demand for security—perhaps the most important single development of the decade. It has shown itself in demands for old age pensions, seniority rights, severance pay, unemployment compensation, and purchase of insurance.

One may ask why there was not a similar demand for security in previous long-drawn-out depressions as in the 1870's and the 1890's. There may have been several reasons, among them the closer proximity to the land. In the 1870's the frontier was still open, and the unemployed might go West and take up homesteads. In the 1890's, there was a return to the land as many unemployed workers returned to the farms as farmers, hired hands, or as "guests" of relatives. Again, in the short depression of 1921, a considerable number of unemployed workers returned to the land. But in the 1930's there was an overproduction of farm products and the Agricultural Adjustment Administration was curtailing acreage, thus making it undesirable to return to the land. Perhaps of equal or greater importance, fewer unemployed workers had any contacts left with the soil or tillers of the soil.

The "farm problem" continued through the 1930's. First the Federal Farm Board was established, with $500 million to use in buying surplus products and then storing them until they were needed, or exporting them. This might have been successful if the depression had been short. However, the $500 million was spent without raising prices although perhaps it slowed up the decline in prices. During the 1930's the Agricultural Adjustment Administration spent almost $7 billion on its plans for reducing production and for supporting parity prices.

The high-wage theory was widely accepted and was a basic philosophy in the National Recovery Administration, 1933–35. According to this theory, purchasing power could be increased by raising wages. However, raising wages when there is widespread unemployment is a very peculiar way of increasing employment since the higher wages furnish a direct incentive for owners to install labor-saving machines. Thus, as far as aiding recovery was concerned, the NRA was a fiasco.

The National Recovery Administration asked members of industries and trades to come to Washington and agree to codes of "fair competition." Under such an agreement, employers must raise wages and agree to collective bargaining, in return for which they could insert in the codes various provisions for controlling or raising prices. Since consumer purchasing power was low—below productive capacity of the economy—the various devices for raising prices were largely ineffective. Within two years, code provisions were so widely ignored that they were practically inoperative before the law was allowed to lapse in 1935. However, it is important to note that the NRA codes marked the beginning of the rise to power of the labor unions.

During the 1930's, many states passed resale-price maintenance laws, allowing sellers to name the prices at which buyers would resell their goods. Several states also passed price floor or "unfair practice" acts prohibiting dealers from selling goods below cost or below minimum markups. Laws which prohibited dealers from selling goods below invoice cost plus cost of doing business (operating expenses) clearly gave the low-cost operator an advantage over a high-cost operator; however, the latter was often given the right to meet competitors' prices. Such laws were too complicated to be enforced.

In 1936, the controversial Robinson-Patman Amendment was added to the Clayton Act. The provisions of this amendment have continued to be widely discussed by students of marketing and by sellers of goods in interstate commerce.

Thus it can be seen that not only did the various laws and government agencies operating during the 1930's fail to solve the problems, but apparently they actually hindered recovery. Per capita disposable income adjusted for price changes was the same in 1939 as in 1929. On the other hand, in previous decades which had severe depressions, the *real* per capita income increased. For example, it increased 30 percent during the 1870's; 20 percent in the 1890's; 14 percent in the 1900's; and 5 percent in the 1920's, in spite of the fact that it was measured from the boom year of 1919. According to estimates of the distribution of income (Brookings and Macfadden), a larger proportion of the families were in the low-income brackets in 1939 than in 1929, with 32 percent under $1,000 and 69 percent under $2,000, as compared with 21.5 and 59.5 percent, respectively, in 1929.

CHAPTER III

The Pioneer Scholars

Beginnings

There was a great increase in higher education beginning around 1900. Prior to this time college education had been very largely for those preparing for the learned professions of theology, medicine, and law. The idea of higher education for businessmen had its beginnings in the closing decades of the nineteenth century. The Wharton School had been established at the University of Pennsylvania, and several other universities had considered or had established schools of commerce (Washington and Lee, Tulane, and Chicago, for example). However, these early schools taught primarily economics, political economy, and sociology rather than commerce or business as the term is now understood.[1] The New York University School of Commerce, Accounts, and Finance, established in 1900, claims to have been the first real school of commerce. Other universities established courses in commerce or schools of commerce in the following years (Illinois in 1902). Several schools of commerce or business were established about 1908 (Denver, Harvard, Pittsburgh, and Northwestern, for example).

Marketing itself came to be recognized as a separate subject shortly after 1900. Several books and reports appeared that dealt with various aspects of marketing or that contained information on marketing.[2] The International Correspondence School developed

[1] Transportation was taught at the Wharton School in 1893–94. This information was provided from Professor Grover Huebner by Professor Orin Burley (Letter of September 29, 1955, from Professor Orin E. Burley).

[2] See Chapter III for a discussion of Walter Dill Scott, Earnest Elmo Calkins, S. Roland Hall, J. E. Hagerty, Arch W. Shaw, and Paul Cherington. There were numerous books in the business field prior to 1900, including the

courses and texts on advertising and salesmanship in the 1890's and 1900's.[33] The reports of the Industrial Commission appeared between 1900 and 1902, and J. E. Hagerty used Volume VI of these as a text in his early marketing courses at Ohio State University; Harlow Higgenbottom published an elementary book on merchandising and credit in 1902.[69] Emory R. Johnson's *American Railroad Transportation* appeared in 1903, and Walter Dill Scott's *The Theory of Advertising* in the same year. In 1904, Ida M. Tarbell's book on the Standard Oil Company explained its marketing methods. Beginning in 1905, the U.S. Bureau of Corporations issued

---

following (see the Summary of References at the end of this bulletin for publication data):

Adams, Edward F., *The Modern Farmer* (1899).

Atkinson, Edward, *The Distribution of Products* (1885, 1892); *The Industrial Progress of the Nation* (1899); *Taxation and Work* (1892).

Bates, Charles Austin, *Good Advertising* (1896).

Benner, Samuel, *Benner's Prophecies of the Future Ups and Downs of Prices; What Years to Make Money on Pig-Iron, Hogs, Corn, Provisions* (1876 [16th ed., 1907]).

Colwell, Stephen, *The Ways and Means of Payment* (1859).

Emery, Henry C., *Speculation on Stock and Produce Exchanges in the United States* (Columbia University Studies in History, Economics, and Public Law, VII, No. 2 [1896]).

Farquhar, Arthur B., and Henry, *Economic and Industrial Delusions* (1891).

Foster, B. F., *The Merchant's Manual* (1837).

Fowler, Nathaniel C., *Building Business* (1892); *Publicity* (1897).

Freedley, E. T., *A Practical Treatise on Business* (1852).

Greene, Asa, *The Perils of Pearl Street* (1834).

Hadley, A. T., *Railroad Transportation, Its History and Laws* (1886).

Hunt, Freeman H., *Lives of American Merchants* (1858).

Lardner, Dionysius, *Railway Economy* (1850).

National Cash Register Co., *The Primer* (1894).

Newcomb, Harry Turner, *Railway Economics* (1898).

Scoville, J. A., *The Old Merchants of New York City* (1863), written under the pseudonym "Walter Barrett,Clerk."

Terry, Samuel H., *The Retailer's Manual* (1869; 16 editions issued).

Wells, David A., *Practical Economics* (1885); *Recent Economic Changes* (1889).

reports on various industries which described their marketing methods.[139-146]

Apparently the first marketing courses at the college level were offered at the universities of Illinois and Michigan in 1902 and at the University of California a few months later.[27, 84] The teaching of advertising and salesmanship at the college level came a little later, although these subjects had been taught before 1900 in private business schools and by correspondence.[33]

The first teachers in the field of marketing were George M. Fisk, E. D. Jones, and Simon Litman. Fisk and Jones began teaching marketing in the universities of Illinois and Michigan, respectively, in the spring of 1902, and Litman at the University of California some months later. Litman then came to the University of Illinois in 1908, when Fisk left to teach at the University of Wisconsin. After some years at Illinois, Litman decided to specialize in foreign trade which has been his main interest since that time.[3]

J. E. Hagerty, who started teaching marketing at Ohio State University in 1905, was another pioneer teacher who deserves special mention. His article, "Experiences of an Early Marketing Teacher," in the first issue of the *Journal of Marketing* (July 1936) is a "must" for every real student of marketing. When Hagerty began the study of marketing while at the Wharton School in 1899, he had to secure his information by interviewing businessmen, which was the case for most of the early teachers in the field. In addition to these interviews, the early teachers obtained their information from government reports, from trade and business periodicals, and from books on various aspects of business and economics.[69]

However, after 1910 published information on marketing began to increase, particularly after 1919. Arch W. Shaw's article suggesting the functional approach to the study of marketing appeared in 1912; Paul T. Cherington's *Advertising as a Business Force*, in 1913;

---

[3] I knew neither Fisk nor Jones, and I have no information about Jones, but as a student I studied Fisk's book, *International Commercial Policies* (1907). Former students tell me that Fisk was an excellent teacher. Soon after he went to the University of Wisconsin he met an untimely death. Litman, who is a delightful and friendly man, well liked by both students and colleagues, was also an excellent teacher.

both Paul Nystrom's *Economics of Retailing* and Grover C. Huebner's *Agricultural Commerce* appeared in 1915; L. D. H. Weld's *The Marketing of Farm Products*, in 1916; and Ralph Starr Butler's *Marketing Methods* (an elaboration of previous monographs), in 1917.

Following 1915 the university bureaus of business research began issuing reports; trade associations and trade papers gathered and published more information on marketing; and the Federal Trade Commission issued numerous reports. There was thus much more information available and a greatly increased interest in marketing, especially in the colleges of commerce. Some dozen books appeared in the years 1920–25, and by this time "marketing had arrived," meaning that it was generally accepted as a separate field of study with its own literature.

Included as "pioneers" in this discussion are only those men who had at least one publication before 1925. Quite a few of these pioneers are still active in study or research. From the present perspective of thirty-five years, it does not appear that later entrants should be considered as pioneers, although at a future time it is entirely possible that some of these later entrants will be so included.[4]

In this study the author has selected the works of twenty-five pioneers for consideration—eleven teachers and nine business and research men. Making the distinction between the teachers and the business and research men is not easy, since many of the pioneers rotated between these vocations. This is particularly true of those listed as teachers.

Walter Dill Scott did most of his writing while a teacher although he later was engaged in research, consulting, and then administrative work as president of Northwestern University. Ralph Starr Butler spent most of his working life in business, but his pamphlets and books on marketing were written while he was a teacher at the University of Wisconsin. Paul T. Cherington spent his later years as a business consultant and researcher, but his books were

[4] Although I have included as "pioneers" only those who began writing prior to 1925, in the closing chapter I discuss publications which, in my opinion, made notable contributions to marketing thought from 1925 to 1939.

written while he was a professor at Harvard University. C. S. Duncan spent more years in government and association work than in teaching, but his books were written while he was at the University of Chicago. Melvin T. Copeland devoted much of his time to research. Paul Nystrom devoted a considerable part of his working years to research, business, and trade association management, but his books were written while he was at the University of Wisconsin and Columbia University.

Although perhaps most marketing men think of L. D. H. Weld as a research man for Swift & Company and for McCann-Erickson, his published works which class him as a pioneer scholar appear to have been done largely at the University of Minnesota, although his *The Marketing of Farm Products* (1916) was published during his short stay at Yale.

Thus it would appear that many of the early teachers either left teaching for more remunerative employment, or that they divided their time between teaching and other work.

There was less rotation or division of time between research or business and teaching by those in the former classifications. Horace Secrist did his work as director of the Bureau of Business Research of Northwestern University, although he was also a teacher. Daniel Starch, W. H. S. Stevens, and Charles Coolidge Parlin started their careers as teachers. Stevens liked to teach, and he taught evening classes for many years while he was in government service. Archer W. Douglas was a very popular lecturer with both student and faculty groups, and probably all of the men in this group lectured to academic groups from time to time.[5]

[5] Some readers may think that I should state how I came into the marketing picture. I started teaching marketing at the University of Pittsburgh in the year 1915–16. My qualifications were small. I had previously taught courses in economics, foreign trade, transportation, economic geography, statistics, accounting, and public debating, and attended a class of Ralph Starr Butler's at the University of Wisconsin which contained some twelve or fifteen lectures on marketing. At this time marketing was just one of the subjects which I taught. Transportation was my first love. My affection changed to marketing as a result of two years of marketing research (1917–19) with the Federal Trade Commission in which I studied the wholesale grocery market in New York City; marketing by upstate New York vegetable canners; the

Writers and Researchers, 1900–1916
Walter Dill Scott
(1869–1955)

Walter Dill Scott entered the field of advertising early, and was known also for his work in developing intelligence tests for the Army, his consulting work in psychology and personnel, and his administrative work as president of Northwestern University. In 1915, he called the first meeting of the National Association of Advertising Teachers, which was to grow into the American Marketing Association. For some years, when he was developing his work at Northwestern University, he offered a new course every year, partly to develop his own knowledge of the field. He is said to have offered the first course of collegiate rank in advertising research at Northwestern University in 1908. He early used the recall method in studying the effectiveness of advertising.[6]

Scott had heard of Harlow Gale's work at the University of Minnesota, and he adapted Gale's method of measuring the attention value of advertising.[33] At that time, which was around 1900, the psychology professors considered psychology as purely for the "ivory tower" and felt that it should not be prostituted by serving any practical purpose. When one of his former professors heard of Scott's work, he wrote him reprimanding him for his heresy and threatening "excommunication" if he did not recant and desist. So

---

activities of midwestern canners' associations; the canned salmon industry; the wholesale produce markets in New York, Philadelphia, Harrisburg, and Pittsburgh; the prices of farm operating equipment; the retailing of farm operating equipment; and the restraints of trade among some farm implement manufacturers. I was joint author of three Federal Trade Commission reports: *Canned Salmon* (1919); *Canned Foods: General Report and Fruits and Vegetables* (1918); and *Causes of High Prices of Farm Implements* (1920).

My first book on marketing, *Marketing Methods and Policies*, appeared in 1921 and was revised and enlarged in 1924. In 1924 I joined the faculty of the University of Illinois where I remained until my retirement in 1957.

[6] Although I had heard of Scott through the various phases of his work, I met him only after his retirement. What I record here is largely my recollection of his conversation.

strong was this feeling that one of the first pamphlets published by the Chicago group interested in applying psychology to advertising was authored by a high school instructor. But Scott did not desist from his studies, and the Chicago Advertising Club gave him encouragement and paid him to write articles for its magazine.

Scott wrote a number of books: *The Theory of Advertising* (1903); *The Psychology of Advertising* (1908, 1910, 1912, 1921); *Influencing Men in Business* (1911, 1919, 1928); and among his other books were: *Increasing Human Efficiency in Business* (1911, 1912); with Robert C. Clothier, *Personnel Management* (1923, 1925, 1931, 1941, 1949), 3d ed. with Stanley B. Mathewson and William R. Spriegel; with M. H. S. Hayes, *Science and Common Sense in Working with Men* (1921); and *The Psychology of Public Speaking* (1907; revised, 1926). *The Psychology of Advertising* was revised by D. T. Howard in 1931. Scott also wrote numerous magazine articles, of which "Psychology of Advertising" in *Atlantic Monthly* (January 1904) should be mentioned.

The following are excerpts of value from Scott's *The Theory of Advertising* (1903):

... There should be a theoretical basis for every important practical undertaking; that the leading advertisers were asking for some fundamental principles upon which a rational theory of advertising could be constructed; and that psychology alone seemed able to furnish such principles. . . . Certain well established facts of psychology were discussed and an attempt was made to show the bearing of such psychological facts upon the work of the practical advertiser.

... One of the greatest problems of the advertiser is how to attract the attention of possible customers. Six fundamental rules for attracting attention were: absence of counter attractions (*e.g.*, size, limited numbers of words); intensity of sensation aroused (*e.g.*, color, motion); contrast to surrounding objects; ease of comprehension (advance from known to unknown, illustrations); repetition; and intensity of feeling aroused.[112]

Among the other "scientific principles" presented were: association of ideas; suggestion ("every idea of a function tends to call that function into activity, and will do so unless hindered by a competing idea or physical impediment"); methods of securing action (*e.g.*, return coupon); prolonged advertising campaigns; and adapting argument to the mental processes of the reader.

Most successful advertisement writers have discovered, after costly experience, that there are certain things which it is unwise to attempt. Of these things one is to attempt to move the mind of the buyer suddenly; another is to attempt to crowd many things into a single advertisement; and another to describe goods in technical terms, or terms that are not understood by many who might be induced to become purchasers.[112]

In his *The Psychology of Advertising* (5th ed., 1912), Scott considered such factors as memory, emotion, sympathy, instincts, suggestion, habit, size of advertisements, mortality of advertisers, and the questionnaires used in research.

He credited Professor Ebbinghouse of Germany as the first to find out how rapidly our memories fade. Many others have studied this subject, and the results are fairly well established and definite.

Our memories are at their best two seconds after the experience has taken place. After two seconds the memory fades very rapidly, so that in twenty minutes we have forgotten more of an experience than we shall forget in the next thirty days.... What we remember a day is a very small part of our experience, but it is the part that persists, as the memory fades very slowly after the first day. What we remember for twenty minutes and what we get others to remember for that time is of great concern, for it is what we and they remember for longer times also.[110]

In addition, four principles were given for improving one's own memory or impressing the advertising message on the memory of readers: repetition, intensity, association, and ingenuity.[7]

---

[7] The memory curve has been used by advertisers in this way: when advertising is begun as when a new product is placed on the market, the advertisements are repeated frequently, and the first ones may be of large size. When the product wins acceptance, the advertisements are used less frequently and may be of smaller size. This is done on the theory that it takes much more effort to place a product in the customers' minds and on the market than to keep it there. Some advertising men will point out that when this is done the product often loses market position. However, the loss of position may be caused by some or all of the following: by failure to keep up with

Scott discussed esthetic values in his chapter on emotions. For example, he pointed out that some shapes are more pleasing than others.

If one dimension of a rectangle exceeds the other approximately sixty per cent, we have the ratio of the "golden section," and the result is more pleasing than in any other ratio of base to height.[110]

Chapter 5 dealt with instincts. "An instinct is usually defined as the faculty of acting in such a way as to produce certain ends, without foresight of the ends, and without previous education in the performance." Instincts, said Scott, tend toward the preservation and furtherance of the interests of the individual. Hence the advertiser directs his appeals to the reader's body (*e.g.*, health, comfort), pleasing foods, the protection and ornamentation of clothes; and to such other instincts as hoarding, ownership (get something "free"), hunting, constructiveness, parental love, companionship, self aggrandizement, moral nature, and curiosity.

In his chapter on "The Psychology of Food Advertising," Scott said that the taste for foods is partially a matter of sentiment and imagination. He pointed out that blindfold tests show that most people are poor on distinguishing one food from another. We prefer turkey to pork and quail to chicken, he said, because they are rarer and because they have a certain atmosphere or halo. Also appearance is very important in our likes and dislikes of foods. He said that the per capita consumption of pork declined 60 percent from 1850 to 1900 while the consumption of eggs increased 85 percent from 1880 to 1900. He attributed this to the more pleasing appearance of eggs.[8] Scott felt that the seller of foods should strive for appearance, elegance, "atmosphere and glamour" in his advertisements, and he should also feature the appearance of the package so that

---

"product development" or improvement, with changes in sales methods, or by the management "just resting on their oars" in other ways, or the philosophy of letting well enough alone.

[8] It may be that the availability of eggs throughout the year to city dwellers resulting from cold storage and better poultry husbandry may well have been an important factor in the increased consumption of eggs. The availability of other meats, the increase in urban population, and increased incomes may have hurt the consumption of pork.

the housewife will remember and recognize it when she visits the grocery store.

Scott presented a study of the mortality of advertisers, in which all advertisements in *Century Magazine* from 1870 to 1907 were examined. The number of pages of advertising per year had increased from 33 in 1870 to 1,056 in 1907. The number of firms advertising during each year varied as follows: 66 in 1870; 293 in 1880; 910 in 1890; 770 in 1893; and 364 in 1907. The average number of lines per advertisement was 38 in 1870 versus 151 in 1907. The number of times a firm advertised per year increased from 4.22 in 1870 to 5.18 in 1893, but decreased to 4.30 in 1907. While the amount of advertising space in 1907 was almost identical with that used in 1890, the number of firms advertising had decreased by 60 percent, while the average amount of space used by each firm had increased by 150 percent.

About the year 1890 the real struggle for existence set in among advertisers, and that is the time we must look for the survival of the fittest. If the small advertisements had been the most profitable, then the users of small spaces would have survived and would have appeared in the following years. Such, however, is not the case. In that fierce struggle the small spaces proved to be incapable of competing with the larger spaces, and we find in the succeeding years that the users of small spaces grew gradually less.[110]

Scott discussed a questionnaire mailed to 4,000 prominent Chicago businessmen to ascertain what papers they read and what interested them most, how much time they spent reading Chicago papers, and what induced them to subscribe to the particular paper or papers they read. The returns on the questionnaire were 57.5 percent. Of these, 14 percent read one paper, 46 percent two papers, and 40 percent three or more papers. Chief interests indicated were local news, political news, and financial news. Sporting news was in seventh place, and cartoons in eighth place. According to the returns, the average businessman spent about fifteen minutes a day reading newspapers. The conclusion was that "the questionnaire method is available in securing data in planning an advertising campaign."[110]

Earnest Elmo Calkins
(1868–   )

Earnest Elmo Calkins, one of the pioneers in developing advertising techniques and literature, wrote several books, including the following: with Ralph Holden, *Modern Advertising* (1905); *The Business of Advertising* (1915); and *Business the Civilizer* (1926); in addition to these works on advertising, Calkins wrote several articles and books of a historical nature.

Calkins is said to have prepared the first complete national advertising campaign. He and his partner, Ralph Holden, prior to 1905, prepared a complete advertising plan

> ... with all phases described, and illustrated with graphs, charts, rough sketches of advertisements for magazines, newspapers, trade journals, posters, window cards, booklets, window displays, all the ingredients that would be used in a complete national coverage, together with publications recommended, estimates of cost of space, methods suggested of merchandising advertising to dealers, accompanied by a running explanation in type-writing, a plan letter, referring to each of the exhibits. The whole presentation was neatly packed in a folding box, appropriately lettered and decorated that added to its novel atmosphere, and incidentally led us to later pioneering in the designing of packages for advertised goods.[156]

This plan was for the Gillette Safety Razor but was never presented to this company. However, representatives of magazines heard of it, and when they saw it were so much impressed that they borrowed it and showed it to various advertisers until it was worn out by repeated handling.

Modern Advertising (1905), written by Calkins together with Holden, is a factual, descriptive, and historical volume of 361 pages, discussing the introduction of many products such as prepared breakfast cereals ("up to 20 years ago the only breakfast cereal available was oatmeal, and up to 5 years ago crackers could be bought only in bulk"), baking powder, and baby food; the various kinds of media (magazines, newspapers, mail, mural—outdoor and car card; up to this time, the H. J. Heinz Company had used only mural advertising); the selection of media; the styles of advertising; the kinds of advertisers (general or national, the retailer, and the mail-order house); the advertising manager; and the advertising agency. The description of the operation of agents in Boston and New York in the 1850's is interesting. The book is quite full of actual examples of advertising representing such products as Sunny Jim (Force); Phoebe Snow (D. L. & W. RR); Sapolio; Royal Baking Powder; W. L. Douglas (shoes); O'Sullivan's (rubber heels); Pears (soap); Pearline (washing powder).

Of particular interest to marketing students is Chapter 3, "The Channels of Trade," one of the earliest treatises on marketing. The typical trade channel was pictured as manufacturer to commission man, to jobber, to wholesaler, through the drummer to the retailer, and hence to the consumers. Calkins indicated that advertising tends to shorten this channel, that the manufacturer can reach the consumer either through the retail stores, or by mail, with the goods being delivered by express or freight. The department store often buys directly from the manufacturer. The dry goods store buys in two ways, either by having its buyers visit the markets or from traveling salesmen, but most dry goods stores can send a buyer only once each season to New York or Chicago. However, some retail stores are owned by the manufacturer. Calkins cited that there were eleven main types of specialty retail stores numbering 205,000. In addition, there were several less important types of specialty stores and 170,000 general stores. He pointed out that during the previous ten years advertising had affected each retail industry—better goods were made than ten years before, partly because increasing prosperity enables people to buy better goods, but more specifically because of advertising. Calkins emphasized that if goods are to be advertised, they must be improved to have qualities to talk about. In this as in other chapters, Calkins gave some emphasis to the need for studying the market or making studies or surveys, although he did not give the methods needed for studying the market.

In his other books, *The Business of Advertising* (1915) and *Business the Civilizer* (1926), Calkins said that advertising costs money, but then so do manufacturing, wholesaling, and retailing. He said that advertising has introduced many new products and greatly ameliorated the work of the housewife; these new products would not have been made if they were not sold. Since advertising increases the sales and profits of sellers, they then pay more taxes. Calkins pointed out that business is a cycle: "A" sells soap to "B"; "B" sells soup to "C"; and "C" sells sealing wax to "A." Advertising can increase sales of individual sellers and can switch sales from one product to another. This idea was further expanded by Collis A. Stocking in his article, "Modern Advertising and Economic Theory," in the *American Economic Review* (March 1931).

S. Roland Hall
(1876–1952)

Correspondence schools were important in developing both courses and books on advertising and salesmanship in the 1890's and 1900's. Among the leading writers of correspondence courses was S. Roland Hall, who was in charge of the advertising courses for the International Correspondence Schools from 1904 to 1913, and who wrote most of its seven volumes which appeared in 1909.[31] These books were widely used, and presumably many of them were utilized as source material by early college teachers.

Nothing comparable to the instruction provided by this course was available in any university in the United States prior to 1915. Hall's treatment had many limitations and several significant deficiencies, but, taken as a whole, it was the best text on advertising procedure written before 1920.[31]

Much of this early material was included in Hall's *Theory and Practice of Advertising* (1926). In addition, he was the author of *The Advertising Handbook* (1921, 1930); *The Handbook of Sales Management* (1924, 1930); *Retail Advertising and Selling* (1924); *Mail-Order and Direct-Mail Selling* (1928); and, prepared especially for home study, *The Fundamentals of Advertising Campaigns* (1935).

Ralph Starr Butler
(1882–   )

Ralph Starr Butler early in his career taught at the University of Wisconsin a course listed as management, for which the text was

Lee Galloway's book *Organization and Management*.[9] However, since Butler seemed little interested in management, the class received more marketing than management from the course. Butler, who was an interesting lecturer, later left Wisconsin for New York University and went on from there to a distinguished business career with the General Foods Corporation.

Butler's *Sales, Purchase, and Shipping Methods* (1911) consisted of 211 pages but was gradually enlarged until in 1917 he published *Marketing Methods*, a clearly presented, well-written work. However, since it had little or nothing on the marketing of farm products and industrial goods, it did not cover the entire field and thus was not a complete text in general marketing. It was, however, the nearest approach to such a text up to this time.

Since chain stores were beginning to attract widespread attention in 1915, Butler devoted some discussion to their method of operation. He felt that chains would have considerable growth in the sale of foods and drugs but not in the dry goods field. About the only example of chains in this field was the J. C. Penney "Golden Rule" stores in which the managers were part owners. It was felt that the problem of selecting goods suited to local needs plus the difficulties of managing stores with such wide and varied stocks would prevent the growth of chains in this field. However, chains have had, in fact, a very large growth in operating stores selling women's dresses, coats, and hats. The ability of buyers continually in the central markets to keep the stores stocked with goods in fashion has outweighed knowledge of peculiar community demands, at least in the popular-priced lines. Automobiles, moving pictures, and increased circulation of magazines and newspapers brought about a greater geographical uniformity in fashions than had prevailed prior to 1915. It is still debated whether central management and merchandising are entirely practical for stores handling the higher priced lines of merchandise. My estimate is that Butler was about eighty percent correct in his forecasts, which is a rather good average for a business forecaster.

[9] In the summer of 1915, I attended Butler's class at the University of Wisconsin.

J. George Frederick
(1882-   )

J. George Frederick was born in 1882, became a newspaper reporter in 1899, and entered the advertising business in 1901. He is currently active in lecturing and writing.

Frederick was managing editor of *Printers' Ink* from 1909 to 1911. In 1910 he and Harry S. McCormack started the Business Bourse, a private marketing research business, and in April 1911 he resigned his position with *Printers' Ink* to devote more time to it. In the 1910's, fees obtained for research were commonly between $10 and $100 but moved up into the thousands of dollars in the 1920's. Frederick said that about 1912 the "Psychology Roundtable" was organized, and then about 1914 the Economic Psychology Association, of which he was the first president. He was a charter member of the New York Sales Managers Club, which was organized in the summer of 1916.[157]

Frederick made several valuable early contributions, among them: *Modern Sales Management* (1919); *Business Research and Statistics* (1920); *Modern Salesmanship* (1925, 1937); *Selling by Telephone* (1928); *Masters of Advertising Copy, Principles and Practice* (1925); and *A Philosophy of Production* (1930). He wrote other books on business.

Frederick's *Modern Sales Management* (1919) was a valuable book deserving further comment. It contained thirty-four relatively short chapters in 393 pages, dealing with both sales policies and the training and supervising of the sales force.[59]

Chapter 1 dealt with the qualifications and duties of the sales manager, while Chapter 2, "Shaping the Product for the Market," said that the article should be the result of sales planning and not sales planning the result of the article. This chapter also said that the market for the article should be analyzed, and cited the case of a $150,000 plant, built to produce an office appliance, which in six months could produce enough goods to satisfy the market for ten years. Frederick pointed out that if the product is new, it should be tested on the market before a sales plan is adopted. He also emphasized the importance of individuality for the product, and the need for market analysis was further emphasized in Chapter 32 on the use of statistics in sales management. He said that the two main classes of statistics are of past performance and of possible developments. Therefore, per capita consumption figures should always be used, and the sales manager should watch for the saturation point of his product.

Chapter 5, which dealt with price making, indicated that the surest way to become independent of a fluctuating market is to develop individuality for the article. However, the price must compare favorably with that of competing products, and if the price is above that of competing products the difference must be justified in the minds of the buyers. A steady price increases goodwill among distributors and the public; however, if there is a likelihood of a change it is well to start with a price that can later be reduced. Quantity discounts, cumulative quantity discounts, discounts for carrying the full line and for sales cooperation, zone prices, resale prices, and proper psychological prices were discussed.

Chapter 6 dealt with the formulation of sound marketing policies. A principle concerns itself with matters of fundamental importance while a policy deals with details of immediate importance, according to Frederick. He felt a seller should have policies regarding price, quality, the guarantee, packaging, growth, financing, accounting, credit, and relations with distributors and competitors. In Chapter 10, in regard to competition, Frederick advocated nonprice competition, especially on giving better service. He felt the company should have a policy toward competition and not leave this to the judgment of individual salesmen. He pointed out that usually it is better to meet competition by having a different policy rather than by using the same policy unless it can be "done overwhelmingly better."

This volume also had chapters on developing a sales organization; setting territories and quotas; selecting, training, and paying salesmen; trade channels; surveys; developing goodwill; creating demand for the product; expense and budgets; and it concludes with the story of an actual selling campaign. The main limitation of this volume was the brevity with which many of the topics were treated. In some cases the treatment was little more than an outline.

Charles Coolidge Parlin
(1872–1942)

The year 1911 was notable in the development of marketing research.[10] Harvard University established its Bureau of Business Research; J. George Frederick started the Business Bourse; General Motors Corporation established its first research laboratory; and Curtis Publishing Company employed Charles Coolidge Parlin to organize a department of commercial research. Businessmen were becoming interested in research and particularly in market potentials and trade areas.

It was Stanley Latshaw's job to find the man to start the research department for Curtis Publishing Company. Latshaw interviewed several men in government bureaus, including the Census Bureau, and then several college professors. None of these seemed to have the proper qualities—they were too much inclined to sit in their offices, and, since the needed information was not in published form, it would be necessary to go out in the field and gather it. Latshaw decided to take a chance on Parlin, who at college had majored in public speaking, had been a high school teacher, and was a successful high school principal. At that time, Parlin knew nothing about either advertising or commercial research, but he was to become one of the leading developers of marketing research.

Parlin was not a conventional scholar, and he left relatively little in published form, though the typewritten reports of his work made a stack higher than his head. Probably his most widely known publications were pamphlets, such as: *The Merchandising of Textiles* (1915); *Selling Forces* (1913); *The Merchandising of Automobiles* (1915); etc.

At the time Parlin went to work for Curtis, it seemed to the managers of Curtis that if a man went out to sell advertising he should know something about the business of the man whose advertising he was soliciting. Advertisers were asking such questions

---

[10] The U.S. Bureau of Corporations had published reports from 1905 to 1913 of various industries including their marketing methods. For a listing of the titles of the various reports see Nos. [139–146] in the Summary of References.

as "What is the possible market for my merchandise? Through what sales channels should I sell? Should I use jobbers? What margins should I allow the jobbers and the retailers? How can I get the dealers to display my merchandise? How much are my competitors spending on advertising?" It was to get the answers to such questions that Parlin was hired. Advertising agencies did not have the answers to these questions. Curtis had recently purchased the *Country Gentleman,* but no one in the organization knew much about the farm market. So Parlin's first assignment was to find out what he could about farm implement manufacturers—where they were located, what they made, how they sold their goods, how much they sold, and what the trade channels were through which the implements reached the farmers. Parlin started traveling, and in the next twenty-five years traveled more than one million miles. He started his new job energetically, and before the year was out, he had compiled an excellent and voluminous report on the farm implement industry. He seemed to have the ability to get businessmen to talk to him and tell him about their businesses.

There were no figures on the volume of sales by department stores. Since Curtis Publishing Company was interested in the kind of goods sold by department stores, Parlin's next assignment was a study of department stores. Stores were visited one by one to find out how they operated and how much they sold. Parlin or members of his staff in 1912 visited almost every city of over 54,000 population and many smaller cities and estimated the volume of department store sales. This resulted in a four-volume report in 1912, and this study was repeated in 1920.

Parlin and his staff found that men and women bought in different ways, and that goods were divided into convenience and shopping categories. Men bought at the most convenient places, by seeking out desired brands, at places where they were attracted by displays, or at customary places where they could charge their purchases. Women were found to buy convenience goods in the same way as men; but, in shopping lines that involved style, women wished to see more than one stock before buying. Thus department stores had grown out of this desire to shop, and it was found that no department store can have a monopoly—the store must have competition. Usually a woman shopped in three stores before buying. Towns of less than 20,000 population were found usually to have just three stores selling style goods to women, but only three cities in the United States had more than seven full-line department stores.[96]

Parlin had to sell the importance of information not only to advertisers but also to his staff of advertising solicitors. He was a good salesman—he made many speeches and his ability as a public speaker stood him in good stead. In line with his high degree of ethical responsibility, his standing instructions to his assistants were: "Go out and do the best job of research you know how to do."[159] Parlin was so much interested in consumer wants and preferences that to him, "The Consumer is King."[2]

Thus Parlin's main contributions to marketing thought were his division of consumer goods into shopping, convenience, and emergency; and his showing to manufacturers and other sellers the importance of consumer preferences. This approach may be said to have been a forerunner of present-day "motivation research."

Arch W. Shaw
(1876–   )

Arch W. Shaw was a businessman with interests in the Shaw-Walker Company and the Kellogg Company. He started the *System Magazine* as a house organ and received so many requests for it that he placed a subscription price on it and developed it into a leading business magazine which became *System, the Magazine of Business*. Shaw also published another well-known magazine, *Factory*, and established a business magazine in England; in addition, he established a company to publish books, particularly business books. This business was later merged with McGraw-Hill Publishing Company, and *System Magazine* may be said to be the parent of the present *Business Week*.

Shaw was invited to Cambridge to help reorganize some of the courses in the Harvard Business School. The organization of the courses had not proven entirely satisfactory and the lecture method was under criticism. It was thought that much of the trouble at the time was (1) there were not enough competent men to teach the various subjects, and (2) it was obvious that more material was needed for the teaching of business. In an effort to help solve this problem, the Harvard Bureau of Business Research was established in 1911 with an announced objective of securing information for use in teaching. Shaw indicated[11] that perhaps a more important object in establishing the Bureau was the hope of gathering information which would enable small business concerns to compete more successfully with large companies. Shaw, like many others, was much perturbed over the growth of large corporations and feared that they would secure too large a share of the market for the maintenance of a healthy economy.

When asked how he developed the idea of the use of functions in the study of marketing, Shaw said that the idea of marketing functions evolved slowly, that he felt a science must be based on a concept, and that there was constant change. Putting these ideas together he said that "marketing is matter in motion." Someone said to him that that is what the universe is. He replied: "I don't care, that is what marketing is—matter in motion." Recalling these days, Shaw wrote:

The immediate purpose of what I was doing was to find a concept around which a philosophy of business could be developed as a basis for a curriculum for a school of business administration and in the article ["Some Problems in Market Distribution"] in the *Quarterly Journal of Economics* for August, 1912, I used marketing as an illustration of the application of such basic philosophy to one of the three types of business activity....[160]

On one occasion, Shaw was preparing a lecture for a class in English economic history in which the assignment had to do with English middlemen. In thinking out his approach on what these middlemen did, he came up with the idea of the functions of middlemen. When this was developed into an article, the functional approach to the study of marketing was born. In saying that "mar-

---

[11] Shaw financed the Harvard Bureau of Business Research for a time. Seldon O. Martin was the first director and held this position until 1916.

keting is matter in motion," Shaw reasoned that the performance of the marketing functions moves the matter through the trade channel to the consumers.

Shaw recognized the following functions of middlemen: (1) sharing the risk; (2) transporting the goods; (3) financing the operations; (4) selling (*i.e.*, communicating ideas); and (5) assembling, assorting, and reshipping. Shaw pointed out that functional middlemen, such as banks, insurance companies, and transportation agencies may take over parts of some of these functions from the middlemen.[129]

Shaw's article "Some Problems in Market Distribution," published in the *Quarterly Journal of Economics* (August 1912), proposed the use of functions in studying the operation of middlemen. This article was then expanded in 1915 to a book published by the Harvard University Press, and contained Shaw's philosophy of business. Both this book and *An Approach to Business Problems* (1916) have profoundly affected the thinking of students of business and marketing.

In his book, *Some Problems in Market Distribution,* Shaw said that business had no scientific body of principles although it has some worthwhile generalizations from economics, such as, for example, the law of diminishing returns—if a larger and larger number of salesmen are placed in a territory, the number of orders will increase but the additional orders may be secured at increasing cost. Business also has rules laid down by successful concerns from observation and experience. Rules of thumb should be replaced by a searching study of all activities of distribution by government, private agencies, universities, and trade associations.

Shaw further emphasized that since motion is common to all business operations, business should study the use of motion and strive to eliminate purposeless motions.

He considered that business is divided basically into three operations: production (change of form); distribution (change of place and ownership); and facilitating operations (financing, credit, collections, purchasing, employment, accounting, auditing, record keeping, statistics, and office management).

Distribution, as Shaw explained it, is divided into demand creation and physical supply. Demand creation must communicate to the consumer's mind such ideas about the product as will arouse his desire and willingness to pay the price. But this demand would be worthless unless the goods could be gotten to him. Demand creation is largely a problem of applied psychology, but ideas about the goods are tangible things, and their results can be measured accurately. Every selling point that proves itself under test becomes so much inexhaustible material that can be used over and over.

The agencies for communication of these ideas are middlemen, the direct salesmen, and advertising. Then the problem, according to Shaw, is to find which of these is best, or which combination is best. Although advertising may be used to create demand and wholesalers and retailers used to get the goods to the consumer, does this method cost too much? Shaw said that there was a definite drift toward a shorter channel of distribution, but the elimination of the middleman is not conclusive evidence that goods would be distributed more economically. For specialties, maximum sales are impossible without advertising or direct selling. If the quality is not evident at a glance, or if it is unfamiliar to the trade, it is difficult to transmit the necessary ideas through middlemen. On the other hand, a "bettered" staple can be sold easily through middlemen. Shaw divides demand into three classes: expressed conscious, unexpressed conscious, and subconscious. He also feels that business has external problems: public opinion, the law, and the government (*e.g.*, I.C.C. and Department of Justice).

Shaw pointed out that sales may be made in bulk, by inspection, by sample, or by description. While sales may be made easily by salesmen in areas with dense population, direct selling may be unprofitable in areas with sparse population. Business needs specific study to determine whether the best results are obtained from salesmen, from direct-mail advertising, or from periodical advertising. Direct-mail advertising can be tested on different groups of prospects, and by different pieces of copy until the best piece of copy and the best groups to circularize are found. However, since consumer groups vary, the copy may need to be different for different groups of prospects.

Further to illustrate Shaw's philosophy of business, the following quotations have been selected from his book, *An Approach to Business Problems* (1916):[128]

When a workman in a factory directs the cut of a planer in a malleable steel casting, he is operating on a piece of raw material for the purpose of changing its form.

When a clerk in a store passes over the counter to the consumer a package of factory-cooked food, his operation is one that results in change of place.

When a typist at his desk makes out an invoice covering a shipment of merchandise, he is operating, not to change the form of matter or the place of commodities, but to facilitate these changes.

Isolate any phase of business, strike into it anywhere, and the invariable essential element will be found to be the application of motion to materials. This may be stated, if you will, as the simplest general concept to which all the activities of manufacturing, selling, finance, and management can ultimately be reduced.

Starting with this simple concept, then, it becomes evident that we have an easy and obvious basis for the classification of business activities. With the philosophical aspects of the concept itself I am not here concerned. Sufficient that it gives us a simplifying, unifying principle from which to proceed, instead of a mere arrangement by kind or characteristic, of the materials, men, operations, and processes which we see in the various departments of a business enterprise.

The nature of the motion does not of itself supply the key to a useable classification. For while the action may be characteristic of one part of a business and not duplicated elsewhere, like the pouring of molten metal in a foundry or the making up of a pay roll, it may, on the contrary, be common to all the departments into which the organization is divided, like the requisition of a dozen lead pencils or a box of paper clips. It is not until we single out the common fundamental element and inquire "What is the *purpose* of this motion?" that we find the key.

I do not wish to exaggerate the importance of this simple and apparently obvious idea; but for me it has opened a way to locate the activities of business and disclose their relations to one another and to their common object, and so has proved a thing of daily use. For the final function of the classification, as it is the practical problem of all business, is to find those motions which are purposeless, so that they may be eliminated, and to discover new motions of sound purpose, that they may be introduced.

Paul T. Cherington
(1876–1943)

Paul T. Cherington, who for some years was at the Philadelphia Commercial Museum and was then called to Harvard to develop the work in marketing, was known by his students as an excellent teacher and scholar.[12] However, Cherington left teaching in the early 1920's for commercial work in which he spent his later years.

Cherington's *Advertising as a Business Force,* a book of readings, appeared in 1913 and came as close to filling the need for a marketing text as any book available at the time. His *The Elements of Marketing,* published in 1920, was extremely helpful to many of the early marketing teachers, primarily because he used the functional approach in organizing his material. Another work for which he received much praise was *The Wool Industry* which was published in 1916. Much later, in 1935, came *People's Wants and How to Satisfy Them.*

Advertising as a Business Force was intended primarily as a text. The selections were from *Printers' Ink* and other business periodicals. Cherington wrote introductions to the various chapters, connective paragraphs, and provided review questions and problem questions at the ends of the various chapters.

Its basic approach or thesis was that advertising is an integral part of selling and that more accurate knowledge is needed as a basis for advertising effort. The material dealt almost exclusively with the problems of marketing manufactured goods reaching the consumer through retail stores. It dealt with such problems as selection of media, jobber and retailer margins, pricing and resale-price maintenance, trademarks, advertising costs, the advertising managers, the advertising agency, and the various selling problems of manufacturer, jobber, and retailer. It was stated that the total

[12] I recall hearing him talk at Atlantic City in 1923 to the National Association of Advertising Teachers. He was given one of the warmest receptions I have ever known an academic group to give a member. As I came to know Cherington, I found the reason. He was one of the kindest and most helpful men I have ever known. He probably answered all letters from students wanting help on term papers.

expenditure for advertising in 1910 was estimated at $616 million of which $250 million went to newspapers, and $100 million to direct mail.

In Chapter 1, Cherington cited the case of a canner of baked beans who advertised well but had a very small increase in his sales. An analysis of the market showed that he needed to increase the consumption of beans, rather than to promote his own brand. When he changed his advertising theme, his sales increased.

In his introduction to Chapter 2, Cherington pointed out that there are two main steps in the distribution of goods for retail consumption. In the first step, the goods are moved in bulk to distributing centers and held there ready for sale and delivery to retailers. This service may be performed by wholesalers, jobbers, or commission merchants.[13] In the second or retailing step, the goods are divided into small units and pass out of trade. This chapter dealt largely with the distributive system and particularly with the changing status of the jobber, with the tendency of the manufacturers to sell directly to the retailers, and of the jobbers to develop their own brands.

After a generation or two of absolute control over the retailer, it would, perhaps, be expecting too much to expect them all to renounce their claims to supremacy. . . . Complaints arise from many quarters that the jobber is too dictatorial and that he ought to be shown that he is not the indispensable fellow he thinks he is. But efforts to oust him are as certain as fate to be fought bitterly and skillfully.[64][14]

In the chapters on "Resale Price Maintenance," Roy W. Johnson, of the *Printers' Ink* staff, argued that advertised articles can be sold at lower expense than nonadvertised goods. Or, stated another way, advertising is a lower-cost method of selling than is personal salesmanship. A retailer said:

We can reduce the cost of doing business very materially by selling price-fixed goods. A boy or girl at a salary of $3 or $4 a week can sell

[13] This step has been called by later students the "intermediate sort" and the "depot theory."

[14] National advertising was undoubtedly affecting the distribution of goods and increasing the power of the advertising manufacturer over both jobbers and retailers.

advertised, price-fixed goods as well as the high priced salesmen; thus the retailer reduces his cost of doing business.[3]

Cherington gave five pages of prices to the retailer, prices to consumers, and retailers' margins on hardware, foods, drugs, and sporting goods to show that price-controlled (maintained) goods are handled by retailers on lower margins. Simple averages of the margin percentages showed 28.9 percent on twenty-eight price-maintained articles, and 30.4 percent on ninety-three nonprice-maintained articles.

L. D. H. Weld
(1882–1946)

L. D. H. Weld contributed much to the development of marketing and deserves a place among the top pioneer scholars. He had a keen mind; and he was reserved, aggressive, energetic, and industrious.[15] During the time he was a member of the staff of the University of Minnesota he made several valuable studies of the marketing of farm products. After leaving Minnesota, he went to Yale for a short time before going with Swift & Company as head of its commercial research department, and subsequently he went with the McCann-Erickson advertising agency where he continued his research and writing for several years.

Of special interest in this study are Weld's contributions: *The Marketing of Farm Products* (1916); and two articles, "Marketing Functions and Mercantile Organizations," which appeared in the *American Economic Review* (June 1917), and "Marketing Agencies Between Manufacturer and Jobber," which was published in the *Quarterly Journal of Economics* (August 1917).

Weld's *The Marketing of Farm Products* (1916) probably influenced the early teaching on the marketing of farm products more than any other single book. It was widely used and some teachers continued to use it for some time even after its revision to *Market-*

---

[15] He impressed me as having a great deal of self-confidence, although some might say he was egotistical. He was a hard man to get acquainted with; I never felt that I really knew him.

ing Agricultural Products by Fred Clark appeared in 1932. It was one of the more analytical of the early books.

In this book Weld suggested that the interest in the marketing of farm products "is undoubtedly due largely to the unusual increase in prices since 1900."[153] He cited that retail prices of food increased 54 percent to 1912 from the 1890 to 1900 average while weekly earnings of laborers increased only 32 percent. This spread took place largely after 1907 and resulted in great interest in the cost of marketing. Marketing, according to the professional economists, is a part of production since it is a part of the productive process. Production is the creation of utilities which are of four kinds—form, time, place, and possession. Of these, marketing deals with time, place, and possession utilities. In this sense, then, production has two major parts: (1) manufacturing and farming, and (2) marketing. The growing interest in marketing, he felt, was centered on the marketing of farm products rather than the marketing of manufactured products, although the latter is often more costly. This public interest arose from the large proportion of income going for food and because of unrest among farmers.

Weld said that if each farmer were self-sufficient, there would be no marketing problem. But, as people became concentrated in cities and as farmers specialized in production, marketing problems began to arise. As marketing becomes more intricate, specialization develops. Weld divided this specialization into two kinds: (1) specialization by commodities, and (2) specialization by functions. For example, butter and eggs were usually handled by the same dealers, but poultry by a separate class of merchants, and in New York City the trade was still further divided between live poultry and dressed poultry. Potatoes were commonly handled by a separate class of traders from other vegetables and fruits. Weld also indicated specialization by function. Roughly he showed marketing to have four successive steps: (1) country shippers, (2) transportation companies, (3) wholesale dealers, and (4) retail stores. In each step there may be two or three successive middlemen (as in the wholesale trade there are the broker, wholesale receiver, and jobber) each performing separate functions. Specialization then becomes a form of division of labor which is desirable because it reduces the cost.

When the statement is made that there are too many middlemen, said Weld, it may mean that the process of subdivision has gone beyond the point of usefulness and that there are too many successive steps; or that there are too many middlemen of each class. Whether or not there are too many successive steps, said Weld,

> . . . it is at least true that there is ample justification for a subdivision of the marketing process among specialized classes of dealers; that in some cases lower cost and greater efficiency may be gained by further specialization; and that in other cases it may be possible to reduce the cost by combining the functions of two or more middlemen into the hands of a single middleman. . . . The problem is to find the most economical combination of functions. This is a matter that can be determined only by careful investigation in each separate trade. . . . On the whole the system of marketing that has developed is efficient, rather than "extremely cumbersome and wasteful," and that there are very good practical reasons for the form of organization that has developed.
> . . . Whether there are too many country buyers, too many wholesalers, or too many retailers, is principally a problem of large-scale production, or proper size of business units.[153]

In regard to country shippers, said Weld, there are often too many as

> . . . the larger the shipping unit, the lower the cost of handling. . . . In the wholesale trade we already have fairly large business units, and it is questionable whether much would be gained by further concentration.[153]

Of produce exchanges he said: "On the whole they represent the highest type of marketing efficiency that has been reached."

According to Weld, retailing is the most expensive step in the marketing channel. The high cost of retailing, he felt, comes from the necessity of the retailers carrying a wide assortment of goods, the habit of the consumers in buying in small quantities, and the services demanded by the consumers, such as credit and delivery. Nevertheless, the cost of retailing groceries (then 16 to 18 percent expense) was at that time less than that for most types of manufactured goods. It is commonly said that there are too many retailers, and yet the expenses of large downtown stores are higher than those of small neighborhood stores. It would not then appear, said Weld, that concentration of business into the hands of larger retailers would reduce costs. Weld pointed to the growth of chain grocers' stores in the East, who reduced expenses by performing their own wholesaling (integration) through buying in large quantities, by doing a cash business, by standardization of the goods handled and their equipment, by savings in advertising and delivery, and by concentrated management. They, however, operated small stores and not large downtown stores. "They mark the most important recent development in the retail grocery field, and the indications are that the movement is destined to spread. . . ."[153] On the other hand, Weld saw very little to be expected from consumer cooperative stores.

He further said:

Substantial reduction in marketing costs lies in the hands of the consumers. If they are willing to buy in larger quantities, pay cash, and carry home their goods they may be able to effect considerable savings in price.[153]

As to improvements in marketing, Weld thought there was hope from farmers' cooperatives, from intensive studies of marketing individual commodities from education particularly at the college level ("the fundamentals of marketing should be taught in every elementary economics course"), and from some state and federal regulatory laws such as, for example, those regulating commission merchants.[153]

Weld's article, "Marketing Functions and Mercantile Organizations,"[152] clarified and expanded Shaw's treatment of functions. Since Weld made the functional concept more usable, his article probably has been more widely used than Shaw's by both students and teachers. He recognized seven functions: assembling, storing, risk assumption, financing, rearrangement (sorting, packing, dividing), selling, and transportation. Another article, "Marketing Agencies Between Manufacturer and Jobber"[151] made a definite contribution to the factual information on marketing methods and channels. Weld also made several studies on the marketing of farm products while still a member of the staff of the University of Minnesota, but the Minnesota farmers did not like to hear the Chicago Board of Trade praised as an efficient market institution, preferring instead to blame it for low prices of grain.

Soon after Weld started work with Swift & Company, the big packers were accused by the Federal Trade Commission of divers and sundry methods of restraining trade and limiting competition.[16] Weld became one of their leading spokesmen and defenders, for which he was widely criticized.[17] According to some of the academic men, it was one thing to engage in commercial research but quite another to become an apologist and defender of companies that are guilty of unfair competition. The code of ethics of the economist is quite different from that of the lawyer.[18]

Wheeler Sammons
(1889-1956)

Wheeler Sammons made a definite contribution in publishing operating expenses of retailers and other factual information about business. His articles, "Keeping Up With Rising Costs," which appeared in the *System Magazine* in the 1910's along with other studies were extremely valuable to businessmen and teachers.[19] He had the capacity for getting businessmen to tell him about their businesses and to give him information often considered "confidential."

---

[16] After the Federal Trade Commission found the "black book," the packers agreed to the famous consent decree. To me this was proof that the Government had evidence of law violations.

[17] Some said that "he sold his soul for filthy lucre." He was reported to receive a salary of $15,000 a year at a time when $3,000 was a really excellent salary for a college professor. Perhaps the professors were jealous.

[18] Personally I felt and still believe that Weld was conservative in his doctrines and philosophy and sincerely believed that the efficiency of the meat packers more than outweighed any sins in restraining competition. It was generally believed at the time that the branch house distributing system of the packers was the most efficient then in existence. Nevertheless I feel that his participation in the packer case hurt his professional standing.

[19] Personally, I was greatly indebted to these articles in *System*.

Businessmen were much concerned about increasing wage and salary rates, and other expenses.[20]

In addition to these articles, Sammons published a book, *Keeping Up with Rising Costs* (1915). In the same year he published *How to Run a Retail Business at Greater Profit* (1915), and he edited *Making More Out of Advertising* (1919). Also for several years he was the publisher of *Who's Who in America* and various other publications of this type.

Paul Nystrom
(1878–   )

Paul Nystrom is considered one of the top pioneer marketing scholars. An excellent student, after securing his Ph.D. degree from the University of Wisconsin, he went to the University of Minnesota for a few years. He then entered private business, established the Retail Research Association, and was one of the organizers of the Associated Merchandising Corporation. The list of members for these two organizations is almost a "Who's Who" among department stores.

Nystrom then returned to teaching as a distinguished professor of marketing at Columbia University. He also became president of the Limited Price Variety Store Association. Although both of these were full-time jobs, Nystrom held them both to the satisfaction of his employers and also found time to deliver several lectures each year before business groups.[21] A man of tremendous energy and capacity for work, Nystrom found time to write several books among which was *Economics of Retailing* (1915), a landmark in marketing literature and knowledge. Among his other books were *Economics of Fashion* (1928) and *Economics of Consumption*

---

[20] Expenses usually lag behind prices in periods of rising prices. However, the merchant who makes little use of machinery may have a problem in controlling his percentage of expense. It is significant that it was during this period (1908–1915) that the cash-carry grocery store came into existence and the Chicago mail-order houses experienced a rapid growth.

[21] I understand that he also operated a farm and for some time helped to operate a large restaurant.

(1929), both excellent books. He then enlarged his *Economics of Retailing* in 1930, and his *Fashion Merchandising* appeared in 1932.

Nystrom's *Economics of Retailing* (1915) was an outstanding pioneer work.[22] In it, he presented rather detailed figures of retail operating expenses. He also showed the importance of the consumers to retailers—their number, incomes, age, sex, and race or nationality—and indicated how their demands change and the importance of this to retailers.

He presented a practical treatment of rent and location of retail stores showing that the percentage cost of rent increased for the better locations in a city and also for the best locations in larger towns as compared with the best locations in smaller towns. According to Nystrom, the best merchant gets the best location since he can use it more profitably; the landlord benefits from unearned increment but he also suffers when the value of his location decreases as is often the case. This theory is compatible with the dictum that rent is price determined and not price determining.

Nystrom showed that the number of retail stores had increased faster than population since 1850 but not nearly as fast as the volume of goods marketed, so that the average store of 1910 sold more goods than the average store of 1850.

Nystrom made a pioneer study of retail failures. He pointed out the two definitions of failure: (1) Reported by Dun & Bradstreet agencies are those failures which represent liquidation of a business with loss to creditors (provided the business is of sufficient size to be reported by these agencies) or insolvency; failures of this kind in any year are less than one and one-half percent of those in business and in most years less than one percent. (2) These agencies, however, remove some 20 percent of the names from their lists each year. Nystrom defined failure as discontinuance of a business because of inability to make it yield a fair wage to the manager and a fair rate of interest on the capital, and it is this latter

[22] I think that this was a development of his doctoral thesis at the University of Wisconsin. I was told by men studying at Wisconsin that Nystrom passed one of the very best Ph.D. examinations in economics of any candidate up to that time.

type of failure that he discussed. He quoted authorities as far back as 1840, saying that only 2 to 4 percent of merchants succeed or acquire independence; that 20 percent of new merchants go out of business within five years, 40 percent within ten years, and 60 percent within fifteen years; or that 10 percent of the men who go into business succeed, 50 percent vegetate, and 40 percent fail.[94, 80, 88]

Nystrom made studies of failures among retailers in his home town of Oshkosh and in other Wisconsin towns from city directories. Of the retailers in business in Oshkosh in 1890, 37 percent dropped out by 1895, 28 percent more by 1900, and 22 percent more by 1910. Thus at the end of thirty years only 13 percent of the original stores remained in business. Similar results were obtained from the studies in other towns. He also studied the causes of business mortality and found them to be as follows: death and illness, 12 percent; sold at loss, 14 percent; sold at profit, 9 percent; bankruptcies, 3 percent; and failures or fizzles, 62 percent. The latter group comprises men who come into business with a small capital, spend a few years struggling hard to make the business go, and then slip out with little or nothing of their original capital left. Most of these failures are closed out in a quiet, informal way with little or no publicity. Nystrom quoted other studies showing the causes of failures (or exits) of retailers to be incompetence (inexperience, laziness, dishonesty, unwise extension of credit, poor locations, extravagance, intemperance, etc.), 50 to 55 percent; lack of capital, approximately 30 percent; and other causes more or less beyond the control of the retailer (sickness, death, fraud, failure of others, and calamities such as fire, flood, robbery, etc.), 15 to 20 percent.[94]

Nystrom believed failures to be higher in retailing than in any other line of business. He concluded, therefore, that retailing was at least in part a parasitic industry since more capital was put into it than was taken out.

Later and more comprehensive studies have found that the failure rate was about the same among manufacturers, wholesalers, and service trades as among retailers. It would, therefore, appear that if retailing is a parasitic industry so are the other industries—

a conclusion that is scarcely tenable. However, as far as his facts concerning the rates and causes of failure are concerned, Nystrom's findings were sound and were supported by later studies.

Nystrom felt that one of the great evils of the marketing system was price discrimination, with such discrimination resulting from inside prices, quantity discounts, free deals, gifts, and the like. Nystrom felt that all sellers should be compelled to sell to all buyers on equivalent terms and thereby prevent cut-throat competition. This proposal was prophetic of the passage of the Robinson-Patman Amendment some twenty years later. In other words—let the retailers buy at the same price and then "let the best man win."[23] Nystrom also advocated resale-price maintenance.

Nystrom felt that a great weakness of the marketing system was that producers were handicapped by expense and often an actual inability to get their goods into retail stores. He therefore proposed that retailers be required to accept goods from all manufacturers on consignment. He felt that this would decrease the cost of traveling salesmen, reduce the cost of distributing goods, and enable manufacturers to reach the consumers. It would then place the risk on the manufacturers "where it belongs."[941]

Nystrom opposed the growth of chain stores, feeling that they would duplicate the existing retail system without returning compensating advantages to the consumers. It is interesting to note that he later worked for many years for a chain-store trade association.

Nystrom opposed also the licensing of retailers, saying that we do not have the necessary knowledge to do so intelligently. He felt that "the problems of distribution are too big and too complex to be solved by simple formulas."

Other subjects he treated included: retail salespeople and their work, and their wages; types of retail stores; taxes on retailers; and methods of fixing retail prices (cost of goods, operating expenses, "what the traffic will bear," competition, custom, salesmanship, and ethics).

Nystrom proposed an ideal retailing system:

---

[23] One may ask if the same should not apply to wholesalers and manufacturers.

The fact that the present system is a product of evolution is presumptive proof that it is far from perfect. Evolutionary movement is always preceded by necessity. Conditions demand a readjustment long before the readjustment takes place. . . . There is a demand, potential at least, at the present time for a retailing system that will supply each community with what the people want, in the way they want it, when they want it, and at the lowest possible cost.[94]

According to Nystrom, the ideal system would have, in addition to the prohibition of price discrimination, the allowance of resale-price maintenance, and the privilege of manufacturers and jobbers consigning their goods to any and all retail stores, salesmen who could give expert service, stores that are sanitary and attractive, and goods that are laboratory tested so that the consumer will have accurate information about them. He felt that untruthful advertising should be outlawed, and he also indicated that the costs of distribution were too high. To reduce them and to attain the other desirable objectives, Nystrom advocated that more statistics should be gathered by the federal and state governments; that more scientific study and education were needed; and that scientific study should be carried out by the retailers and their salespeople. He also pointed out: "Business must be made fit to teach. Machiavelian training has no place in a public educational system."[94]

Since Nystrom's *Economics of Retailing* (1915) was one of the most analytical books appearing during the period under consideration, one should consider some of his major findings, conclusions, and recommendations: His treatment of rent was excellent. He made a pioneer study of retail failures, and his facts were in line with those found by later studies.[24] His statements about price discrimination were supported by studies of the Federal Trade Commission made some years later, and the Robinson-Patman Amendment was passed to try to correct the situation but with not too much success. The present feeling among many market economists is that to stop price discrimination entirely would unduly lessen competition. While resale-price maintenance is still debated,

[24] I cannot, however, agree with his conclusion that retailing was a parasitic industry because more capital went into it than came out of it, since the failure rate was almost as high among manufacturers and wholesalers.

most marketing economists have been and are opposed to it. Chain stores have grown without the bad effects predicted. Nystrom's proposal to require retailers to accept goods on consignment from any manufacturers or jobbers seems impractical although it has not been tried. On the other hand, his proposals for better trained salesmen, for more standardization and testing of goods, for stopping untruthful advertising, for more research, and for more scientific study by both the retailers and the government are almost universally endorsed. On the whole, Nystrom's theories and proposals were sound, but, regardless of how much of his material has been accepted, he presented much information and made many recommendations which aroused interest and stimulated study.[25]

Scholars, 1917–1923
W. H. S. Stevens
(1885–   )

W. H. S. Stevens, who has a Ph.D. in economics and a knowledge of law, specialized in the problems of unfair competition. He was called from Tulane University to the Federal Trade Commission, whose duty it is to prevent unfair competition, and he became one of the outstanding economists with this organization. A human dynamo, Stevens liked to teach, and in addition to his Trade Commission work he taught one, two, or three evenings a week as well as finding time to write a number of scholarly articles. Personally, he is friendly and likable, and when younger had an exceptionally strong voice.[26]

In his work with the Federal Trade Commission, Stevens was responsible for more of their good economic reports than any other one person. He was examiner-in-charge and largely personally responsible for the monumental *Report on the Grain Trade* (1920–1926), which is said to be the best and most complete study ever made of the marketing of grain in the United States. He was exam-

[25] I used this 1915 book as a text in the beginning marketing course in 1915–16 and as required reading for many years in graduate classes.
[26] His friends said: "His whisper could be heard around the block."

iner-in-charge of the investigation and report on *Bakery Combines and Profits* (1927). He and Walter Durand were jointly in charge of the report on *Furniture* (1923); he was examiner-in-charge of the *Investigation of Chain Stores* (1931–34),[51] which was voted by a national jury of marketing scholars to be the most valuable economic study made by the Federal Trade Commission. Stevens was also in charge of many other investigations for which he wrote all or part of the reports.[27] Some of these studies continued for years, and Stevens might have two or three of them going at the same time under his general supervision. After he left the Federal Trade Commission for the Interstate Commerce Commission, there was a dearth of these good economic reports for some years.

Stevens' philosophy is well expressed in his book, *Unfair Competition* (1917):

In an economic sense fair competition signifies a competition of economic or productive efficiency. In other words, an organization is entitled to remain in business as long as its production and/or selling costs enable it to compete in a free and open market.[133]

He pointed out that the more efficient operator usually reduces his price to increase his volume, and that the marginal or high-cost operators will gradually lose their markets. This may seem harsh, but the benefits of competition must be found in its benefits to society. However, he said, competition has not always been conducted in this way:

Efficient concerns have by no means always survived. All too frequently they have been destroyed not by superior efficiency but by methods against which their own efficiency afforded little or no protection. Again and again methods and practices have been employed which destroy the freedom of the market, which restrict and hamper the efficiency of other units, and prevent potential competitors from becoming actual rivals.[133]

Stevens felt that the greatest development and diversification of unfair methods have been practiced by highly monopolistic organi-

[27] The conduct of a Trade Commission investigation involves a great deal of work. Often a staff must be recruited, trained, and supervised; the work planned; and assignments made. Then results must be summarized and analyzed, and reports must be written.

zations. He named twelve classes of unfair competition: local price cutting; operation of bogus independent concerns; fighting instruments; conditional requirements ("tying clauses"); exclusive arrangements; black lists, boycotts, white lists, etc.; rebates and preferential arrangements; engrossing machinery and goods; espionage; coercion, threats, intimidation, etc.; interference; and manipulation. Stevens gave these not as a complete list but rather as illustrations of the unfair methods "which have been and are being employed . . . which are uneconomic and hence unfair."[133]

Stevens rejected the competition theory of monopoly, which holds that large producers have lower costs than small producers and so drive out the smaller producers; then large concerns may combine or the process may continue until only one producer is left. Stevens contended that it is unfair methods of competition and not efficiency that drives out competitors. He said that if consolidations are prevented by the Sherman Law and unfair methods of competition are eliminated by the Federal Trade Commission, then a monopoly can result only from superior efficiency for a sufficient period of years to enable an organization to eliminate competitors.

But there is nothing necessarily continuous in efficiency: rather, the contrary. The efficiency of an organization fluctuates with changes of men in the organization, and with changes in production and selling methods. It is doubtful if a given organization can remain the most efficient long enough to attain a monopoly by elimination of its competitors. It would not only have to attain a monopoly but would have to maintain the highest efficiency to prevent new competitors from entering the field and securing part of the market.[133]

Stevens cited the case of the United States Steel Corporation which did not use unfair methods and which from 1901 to 1911 increased its sales by only 40-odd percent and part of this by acquiring the Tennessee Coal, Iron, and Railroad Company and other companies. In contrast, eight other large steel producers increased their output by amounts ranging from 63 percent (Lackawanna) to 3,780 percent (Bethlehem). The International Harvester Company was not entirely guiltless but used few if any unfair methods after 1907. In a decade its proportion of the market dropped on its main products as follows: 13 percent for binders, 20 percent for mowers, and 20 percent for rakes.[133]

Stevens concluded that if consolidations are prevented and unfair methods of competition eliminated, it is doubtful if the "results of competition will ever extend to the point of actual monopoly."

Archer Wall Douglas
(1858–1935)

Archer Wall Douglas, a vice president of Simmons Hardware Company of St. Louis, was a most interesting man—an excellent lecturer, an expert graphologist, a fascinating conversationalist, and a gentleman of the "old school."

He wrote *Merchandising*, published in 1918, as well as several other books and articles. He wrote two pamphlets published by the Chamber of Commerce of the United States of America in 1919 on the *Relations of Weather and Business*,[147] and also had an article in the Weather Bureau monthly.[148]

In *Merchandising* he explained clearly how to use sales and stock records and other information as a basis of purchasing. He showed how the sales of various articles were affected by changes in weather, fashions, inventions, and living conditions. He felt the buyer should study sales records of all items each time an inventory is taken. Thus if sales are increasing, the quantities purchased should be increased; while if sales are declining, less and less should be purchased and purchases should be stopped before sales cease entirely. For example, the coming of the automobile caused sales of horse collars, pads, hames, trace chains, harness, whips, fly nets, horseshoes, and other horse goods to decline but increased the sales of automobile accessories, attachments, tires, tire pumps, and the like. Likewise, the coming into general use of electricity caused a decline in the sales of the more expensive oil lamps, but caused an increase in the sales of various electrical appliances. The growth in popularity of golf caused a slump in the sales of croquet sets, formerly bought in carload lots ("we called it Presbyterian baseball"), but brought an increase in the sales of golf clubs, golf bags, and golf balls.[28]

In his Chamber of Commerce pamphlets on *Relations of Weather and Business*, Douglas drew some generalizations derived from purely empirical evidence, but he said that his forecasts were correct approximately eighty percent of the time.

"Weather changes and happenings occur in an irregular yet relentless cycle of about thirty-five years." Douglas indicated that the probabilities are that three average wet years will be followed by two drier ones and the drier ones in turn by three or more wetter ones. In an area of low rainfall, he said, the sequence may be two wet years and three dry ones. The months of April, May, and June correspond in the proportion of precipitation to that of the average of the entire year, and thus the businessman has a basis of forecasting summer sales of goods by observing rainfall. For example, a dry March is a danger signal. A dry summer is also a hot summer, and in a dry summer the sales of garden and lawn hose, electric fans, refrigerators, and many other products increase. Also, a dry summer will reduce the size of the corn crop, and the hay crop too. But with more corn cut for forage, the sale of corn knives will be increased.[147]

Douglas also concluded that temperatures affect sales and business greatly. But, he pointed out,

. . . the so-called average, or what are known as "mean" temperatures are worse than worthless for all business purposes as they are thoroughly misleading. Years in which there are the most violent differences in extremes of temperatures show mean temperatures within a few degrees of each other.[147]

Douglas pointed out that for business purposes cold and warm seasons are determined by extremes of temperatures and their duration. For the purpose of the study, he classed winters with a temperature below zero at St. Louis as "cold" and summers with temperatures above 100° as "hot." "There are groups of cold winters, often three or four together, succeeded by more moderate ones, though not so numerously associated." Similarly, he said, two hot

---

[28] Some of these illustrations are taken from Douglas' lectures.

summers come together and are followed by three or four of more moderate temperatures. However, a hot summer does not indicate that it will be followed by a mild winter, but a cold winter is usually followed by a cool summer. Still further, "there does not seem to be any connection between temperature and precipitation in winter."[147] Here again he indicated that temperature has an important effect on the sales of many commodities. For example, in a cold winter more ice skates and sleds will be sold.

C. S. Duncan
(1878–   )

During the academic phase of his career, while he was teaching at the University of Chicago, C. S. Duncan published *Commercial Research* (1919), a pioneer study. However, an examination of the records at the University of Chicago found no evidence that Duncan taught a course in research there. Duncan left academic work and spent several years as an economist for private organizations including the Association of American Railroads.[29]

One of the many interesting features of Duncan's *Marketing: Its Problems and Methods* (1920)[30] was his emphasis on trade information or market news: The world "in its essential business organization still pivots on price and the essence of price is still market news."[40]

In *Commercial Research,* Duncan said:

One large field of research has as yet been practically untouched. This is the domain of buying and selling.... A program of this sort means that the attitude of research, of careful scientific analysis is to be held by the merchant.... Commercial research goes far beyond mere figures.[39]

Yet, he said, "facts from whatever source, of whatever character, are the working material of business research in all its phases."

[29] It is interesting to speculate what other contributions he would have made if he had remained in academic work where he would have been encouraged to conduct research and to write.

[30] In my opinion, this was *the first* reasonably complete text for a general course in marketing.

Duncan's sources of facts included sales records, purchase records, books, trade journals, government reports (particularly those of the Department of Agriculture, Bureau of Foreign and Domestic Commerce, and the Federal Trade Commission, and the Census Bureau), letters of inquiry, and mailed questionnaires.

Melvin T. Copeland
(1884–)

Melvin T. Copeland is one of the outstanding pioneer scholars in the field. A "down east" New Englander, he gives the impression of being shy, and since he attended very few meetings of the American Marketing Association, he was not as well known throughout the profession as he might otherwise have been. He might have had greater influence if he had taken more interest in marketing meetings and organizations. On the other hand, he probably felt he could spend his time to better advantage in research.[31]

Copeland, who became director of the Harvard Bureau of Business Research in 1916, did very valuable work in gathering and publishing information on the operation of retail stores, as well as on other subjects. In later years, he switched to teaching business policies and lost much of his interest in marketing.

Although not the first to use problems in teaching,[32] Copeland's development of the problem method of teaching is probably considered by most students of marketing to be his most valuable contribution. However, his work in the research bureau and his devel-

---

[31] It seemed to me that he partially "hid his light under a bushel." I enjoyed and greatly admired his writings.

[32] I have heard many stories about the development of the problem method at Harvard and of Copeland's teaching. Many who visited his classes reported that he said very little, acting more as a chairman than as an orthodox instructor. I have talked with many of his students and they have told me that they learned a great deal of marketing in his courses. As I understand the matter, he made the students do all the work. Isn't this the best teaching? We learn only by doing and the more work the teacher can induce the students to do, the better teacher he is.

opment of material on industrial marketing were, I think, of greater importance than his *Problems*.

Copeland published several books among which was *The Cotton Manufacturing Industry of the United States* (1912), which had valuable information on problems dealing with the cotton manufacturing industry. The material on the marketing of textiles was excellent and of particular use to marketing teachers in the early years. In 1920 he published *Marketing Problems*, the first of the Harvard problem or case books. Many marketing scholars consider this book, with its short problems, to be the best of them all. In 1923 he published an article, "Relation of Consumer Buying Habits to Marketing Methods," in the *Harvard Business Review* (April 1923), and in 1924 another book, *Principles of Merchandising*. In these, he further developed Parlin's classification of consumer goods and showed its use and importance in the commodity approach to the study of marketing. He outlined buying motives for each type of goods, and his classification and discussion of the marketing of and buying motives for industrial goods was particularly valuable.

Copeland went into some detail to list principal consumer buying motives based on an examination of 926 advertisements in general and women's magazines and in farm papers. He divided motives into (1) primary, or those that arouse the latent impulse to buy a certain article or service; and (2) selective (competitive), or those which induce consumers to buy a specific brand or patronize a specific seller. Then he divided motives further into rational, which appeal to reason, such as economy, dependability, or durability; and emotional, which appeal to emulation, pride, comfort, and the like.[36]

Copeland found the principal emotional appeals to be: pride in personal appearance, personal comfort, emulation, preservation of health, pride in appearance of property, taste, distinctiveness, home comfort, and satisfaction of appetite. Others were: economical emulation, social achievement, proficiency (satisfaction in doing a thing well), romantic instinct, cleanliness, proper care of children, alleviation of laborious tasks, security from danger, pleasure of recreation, entertainment, and greater leisure.

He found the principal rational motives to be: economy in price, dependability in quality, dependability in use, durability, and economy in use. Others were: efficiency in operation, increased productivity, increased earnings, and reliability of service. He also lists patronage motives which induce consumers to patronize a particular retailer or wholesaler—such as quality of goods, reputation or brands of goods handled, reputation of store for fair dealing, personalities of merchants and salesmen, credit, and ownership of stock in company.[36]

Horace Secrist
(1881–1943)

Horace Secrist was director of the Bureau of Business Research of Northwestern University for some years, as well as a member of the faculty of that institution. His students have said that he was an excellent teacher and an outstanding scholar.[33] He gathered operating statements from several groups of businesses, particularly retail stores, and analyzed them carefully and thoroughly. Perhaps because he was so thorough, Secrist seemed to be able to get more information out of a set of operating statements than anyone else.

One of the early writers on statistics, he published *An Introduction to Statistical Methods* [a Textbook for College Students] in 1917 (revised, 1925); and in 1921, *Cost, Merchandising Practices, Advertising, and Sales in Retail Distribution of Clothing* [in five small volumes]. Among his bulletins for the Northwestern University Business Research Bureau were: *A Business Barometer for Retailers* (1922); *Stockturnover in Retail Clothing Stores* (1922); *Commercial Rent as an Expense and Its Relation to Profits* (1923);

---

[33] As one of his students said: "You felt that you *had* to produce. That was the kind of teacher he was . . . but he was rather cold and distant." Another speaks of the logic of his research: "He was a perfectionist in his research and his teaching. He spared no effort in running down the fine points of any subject. Frankly, I think he went too far in this; that he got himself so bogged down in detail" that he never finished some of his studies. Another commented that he was "one of the finest graduate teachers I have ever known. He fed us a continuing flow of inspirational books and ideas. He was a scholar and beyond that an original thinker."

Competition in the Retail Distribution of Clothing (1923); *Expense Levels in Retailing—A Study of the Representative Firm and of Bulk Line Costs in Distribution of Clothing* (1924); *Expense, Profits, and Losses in Retail Meat Stores* (1924); *Margins, Expenses, and Profits of Retail Hardware Stores* (1928); and *A Seven Year View of Sales and Expenses of Retail Clothiers, 1916–1922* (1924). Secrist wrote two other publications of interest, *The Widening Retail Market and Consumers Buying Habits* (1926), and *The Triumph of Mediocrity* (1933).[116-127]

Secrist found that "costs each year are distributed about their average in substantially the same manner. The positions of individuals shift." In his study of the representative firm (following the definitions of Marshall and Taussig), he found that a firm does not stay representative over any great number of years. Taking the mode as all stores with expenses within 20 percent of the average (above or below), he found that only 22 percent of the retail clothing stores studied (analysis made by city size) remained in the modal group for seven years. A study of identical stores showed that a store usually moves its position widely from year to year. It moves in and out of the modal group, and often moves from below to above, or from above to below the average expense figure.[126]

In his *A Business Barometer for Retailers,* Secrist found that

... stores with expenses far above the average tend to move toward the average in subsequent years. Likewise there is a tendency for those with expenses markedly below the average, to move toward the average in the following year. Those whose costs are near the average tend, on the other hand, in subsequent years to move outward from the average.[116]

Thus the dispersion is as great at the end of the period as at its beginning. In his *Triumph of Mediocrity*, these tendencies were expanded for various types of businesses.

Secrist's findings indicated that those businesses with the highest expenses (in the highest quartile) usually reduce them or go out of business. If they go out of business, they remove themselves from the sample of those who report continuously over the period under study. A high-cost operator has a very strong incentive to improve his efficiency to avoid failure. On the other hand, many of those with the lowest expenses (lowest quartile) allow their expenses to increase over a period of years. There may be several reasons for this: (1) perhaps becoming self-satisfied and following the philosophy of "let well enough alone," or (2) the owners growing older and becoming less aggressive or less industrious. These are only a few of the possibilities that might explain Secrist's findings.[34]

In his *Widening Retail Market* (1926), Secrist showed the effects of increased travel by automobile on the purchase of men's clothing. At the time of the study in 1926, the automobile was not only making trade more mobile but it was taking more of it to the retailers in the larger towns.

Fred E. Clark
(1890–1948)

Fred E. Clark was one of the very best of the library-research scholars in the marketing field. His books were carefully written.[35] His contribution was more in digging out, summing up, and clearly presenting existing knowledge than in presenting new theories.[36] His students say that he was an excellent teacher—both as a lecturer and as a stimulator in seminars. One of his students, for example, speaks of "the close friendly relation between student and teacher and his ability to get the class excited about a problem."[37]

Clark was one of the five men who have been elected twice to the presidency of the American Marketing Association,[38] which

---

[34] These are my views. I think that another, and perhaps more difficult, question is "Why do those businesses, with expenses near the average, tend to move away from the average?" Secrist's findings raise questions which have not, in my opinion, received sufficient consideration by students of marketing. Answers to these questions might be of great use to business operators.

[35] Perhaps the fact that Mrs. Clark is a trained librarian helped.

[36] As far as I have been able to discover, he was not interested in field research.

[37] Professor Ira Anderson of Northwestern University.

[38] The name of the American Marketing Association has been changed several times.

shows the high esteem in which he was held by members of the profession.[39]

Clark's *Principles of Marketing* (1922), an excellent book, was one of the very best of the early books.[40] It was widely used and has been revised several times (revised, 1932; 3d ed., 1942, with Carrie P. Clark; reprinted, 1947). In 1932 came his widely used *Marketing Agricultural Products in the United States,* which he wrote with L. D. H. Weld. He also published *Readings in Marketing* (1924) which was revised in 1933. Two articles deserve mention: "An Appraisal of Certain Criticisms of Advertising," *American Economic Review* (March 1925); and "Discussion of Weld's Paper on 'Do Principles of Large-Scale Production Apply to Merchandising?,'" *American Economic Review* (March 1923). In addition, his "Fred Clark's Bibliography as of the Early 1920's" which was published in the *Journal of Marketing* (July 1945) was probably the most complete one possessed by any individual marketing student at the time.[28]

When the *Principles of Marketing* was published in 1922, much was being said about distribution costs being too high. Much of Clark's final criticism in Chapter 26 was devoted to an analysis of this allegation. Advertising in this period was being criticized in particular. Clark defended advertising for its educational value in announcing new articles, explaining their use, and announcing prices. He felt that advertising had other advantages as a cheaper method of selling than personal salesmanship. He said that although criticisms of advertising give the impression that it is a costly method of selling,

. . . the reverse is usually true. For although the use of salesmen is usually considered the more effective method of selling—cost ignored—it is often too expensive. . . . It is generally agreed that advertising in many instances has lowered selling costs as well as manufacturing costs.[22]

---

[39] I do not recall any man in the profession who was so well known and widely liked as was Fred Clark in the 1920's.

[40] Part of the material in mimeographed form was used in his teaching for two or three years previously.

He points out that advertising does this by bringing about large-scale production and smoothing the valleys in demand. He said, "most of the comforts enjoyed today, have been made commercially possible only by sales effort."[22] Thus advertising can switch demand from one seller to another and from one product to another.

Much was being said at that time about there being "too many middlemen." Clark analyzed this charge, quoting Nystrom and following his reasoning in regard to retail stores. There had been considerable growth in chain stores between 1915 and 1922, and Clark saw some hope in them because they combined the advantages of the small store for the consumer with the advantages of central administration and large-scale purchasing.

Clark felt that marketing costs could be reduced by more standardization of consumer goods, which would enable consumers to buy more intelligently. He questioned the social desirability of branded staples which manufacturers used to individualize their products and counteract "competition on a pure price basis," for often there is no real difference in such goods.[22] This idea was put much more strongly by Stuart Chase and F. J. Schlink in *Your Money's Worth*, written in 1927.[15]

Frederick A. Russell
(1886–   )

Frederick A. Russell obtained his doctor's degree at the University of Illinois in 1916, taught for a few years at the University of Washington, and returned to the University of Illinois in 1919 to develop the marketing courses. He started teaching sales management in 1920 and started the graduate program in marketing in 1921. One of the very best teachers and lecturers in the University of Illinois, Russell spent more time in conference with students than most teachers. He was also interested in civic and athletic affairs, and served his profession twice as president of the American Marketing Association.

Russell's *The Management of the Sales Organization* appeared in 1922. This volume dealt with the personnel aspect of sales management—the relation that should exist between the sales manager and his men. The reason for thus confining the discussion was twofold: (1) the determination of general marketing policies had been treated elsewhere; and (2) the human element was growing steadily in importance and presented at that time "what is generally recognized" as the chief problem in the industry of the period. This volume dealt with the selection, training, equipping, stimulating, and compensating of salesmen. It considered the use of contests, conventions, conferences, letters, bulletins, and house organs in training and stimulating them. This exceptionally well-written and usable book made a real contribution to the literature in the field.

Russell's *Textbook of Salesmanship,* which appeared in 1924, received a very high rating by a national jury of marketing scholars. Over the years, this book, and its revisions (3d ed., 1941, with Frank Herman Beach; 5th ed., 1955, also with Beach), has been one of the most widely used texts in college courses on salesmanship.

W. D. Moriarty
(1877–1936)

W. D. Moriarty taught at several schools including the University of Michigan and the University of Southern California.

A teacher of both economic theory and of advertising, Moriarty combined the two subjects in his book, *Economics of Marketing and Advertising,* which was published in 1923. In this unusual contribution, Moriarty expressed his belief that marketing was largely an expression of economic theory. Since this was and is an unusual point of view, the book had only a limited sale as a text. Since the book contains forty-three chapters, it has been necessary to select only a few for discussion here to give something of the "flavor" of the book.[41]

[41] While the student who has taken graduate courses in economic theory and in the history of economic thought may be familiar with much of the background material in this book, he, as well as the marketing student and the market executive, will find many significant interpretations and thus should find the book both interesting and stimulating.

In Chapter 10, Moriarty discussed Say's Law, which explains the often made but little understood statement that supply equals demand: "Say's Law is a fundamental principle, deep in the nature of our present order, which constantly tends to establish the actual equality of demand and supply on the market." In order to explain Say's reasoning, Moriarty stated this law as follows: "The total amount of goods produced *and sold* on the market creates an equal amount of demand on the market, and therefore total supply and total demand must be equal." He made the point that the goods must not only be produced but must be sold to give the producers (workers and entrepreneurs) the demand for other goods: "Men produce for the market in order to demand from the market an equal amount of goods produced by others."[86]

He applied this to nations as well as to individuals, since a nation can demand from other nations only as much as it supplies to other nations:

Just why anyone should think that sending a plow from Moline to Argentine was contributing more to the wealth of the United States than if it were sent to Minnesota to help raise crops there would seem difficult to explain.[86]

Moriarty said that there can be no overproduction as long as the goods are sold, although there can, of course, be an overproduction of specific articles when a producer misjudges the market and makes more than he can sell. Goods, he said, must be produced which others want: "Under our present economic order the only way in which anyone has an economic right to share the general social income is by producing something which others want." Thus, the keen businessman "will exercise his activity in a field where the market needs are most evident. He will not . . . allow his production to outrun the capacity of his sales force." Thus, pointed out Moriarty, if one understands the principles, "he gets a vision of the limitless development of the market impossible to those who have a fear of the bogey of general overproduction."[86]

Moriarty felt that this principle, like other economic laws, operates in the "long run." For short periods, of course, there may be suspended demand and anticipated demand. People produce only to secure power to demand goods, but the time between the securing and exercising of demand normally stays about the same. However, said Moriarty, if there is a great increase in the suspended demand, the exercised demand may not equal the total supply. He pointed out that this may happen if prices are high and a decline is generally anticipated, or if workers fear unemployment. This situation is common, he said, in the beginning of a period of depression and gives rise to the common statement that overproduction causes the depression.[86]

Moriarty, pursuing this point of view, said that there may also be anticipated demand—that is, when a large number of producers buy in anticipation of demand which they expect to produce in the future. This may be done by buying on credit. However, Moriarty said, any unusual suspension of demand tends to make market demand less than market supply and tends to lower price; on the other hand, any unusual utilization of anticipated demand tends to make market demand exceed market supply and raise prices.

Moriarty developed another point which is of great importance in current thinking:

> Economic want includes two things—the desire for a thing and the ability to pay for it. If the desire is great enough the man may get to work and produce something which someone else wants and so get the ability to pay for the thing desired. This is the essential motivation of our present order.[86]

If one applies this thought, he can say that marketing (salesmanship, advertising, etc.) can arouse such strong desire that man works harder and increases his income—that is, marketing can increase income and the demand for goods.

Moriarty explained that time and place utilities are just as real as form utility. In Chapter 22 he said:

> The development of modern methods of production has been dependent on the development of marketing. For large scale production and territorial division of labor, the marketing process is just as essential a factor as the labor employed in the factory. Market analysis is essential in determining both the type of goods it will pay [be profitable] to manufacture and the quantities that can be marketed successfully.[86]

And marketing is necessary to dispose of the goods and to secure the money for further production.

According to Moriarty, marketing creates new value by increasing consumer surplus, with this idea being based on the law of diminishing utility. The wheat farmer who first satisfies his own needs finds this wheat has a high utility to him. However, if he can trade additional wheat for corn or some other good, the wheat he parts with has less (the least) value to him while the good he obtains, since it is the first of that good, has a high value. In this way, marketing increases real incomes, and salesmanship then comes into play to create this surplus.

In Chapter 24, Moriarty discussed the idea that market price records the value to the marginal buyers. He said that the single price fixed in the market gives the total exchange value of all the goods sold at a given time. But, he pointed out, salesmanship, even that of the auction room, increases subjective value to the buyer; and, since the subjective value is above objective or market value, the consumer's utility or satisfaction is increased: "Salesmanship must therefore be regarded as true economic production." In addition, said Moriarty, the salesman is also of value to the buyer in instructing and educating him so that he will use the goods better and derive more satisfaction from them. Thus salesmanship forces the buyers to weigh the relative advantages of various items in their buying budgets, educates them, and helps them develop adequate judgment.[86]

Daniel Starch
(1883–   )

Daniel Starch joined the faculty of the University of Wisconsin in 1908 and beginning in February of that academic year offered a course in the "Applications of Psychological Principles to Advertising," repeating the course each year until 1919 when he joined the Harvard faculty. This early course was "definitely an approach from the research point of view."[161] He finally left teaching to establish his own company, and he developed *Magazine Audience Studies*.[42]

Starch wrote two books which made outstanding contributions to the literature on advertising: *Advertising: Its Principles, Practice, and Techniques* (1914) and *Principles of Advertising* (1923).

Like many of its predecessors, *Principles of Advertising* covered the techniques of advertising—copy, layout, typography, color, headlines, illustrations, and media. In addition, it discussed the place of advertising in business, the research that should precede advertising, the analysis of human nature, and the selection of appeals.

In discussing the history of advertising, Starch traced its development through four stages: (1) preprinting, prior to 1450; (2) early printing, 1450–1850; (3) modern expansion, 1850–1911; and (4) the development of standards of practice and the introduction of research, 1911 to date.

Advertising research may use secondary data (statistical and otherwise), questionnaire surveys, and laboratory and field tests. Starch showed the value of the statistics of population, income, education, sex, and the place of residence. He said that man has certain inherent desires, but the way of satisfying them varies. The seller's business is not to create new desires, said Starch, but to direct these desires in certain directions, stimulate them to action, or show new ways of satisfying old desires. He listed thirty-eight inborn desires or instincts which center around two things: (1) the preservation and comfort of the individual, and (2) the continuity and welfare of the human race. He gave the tentative rating of 44 active motives as made by 74 persons.[43] In this study, he rated hunger the highest with 9.2 out of a possible 10, and teasing with the lowest, 2.6. He discussed methods of determining the value of appeals through field tests. He quoted a preliminary study of 25 New York families by Hollingsworth showing purchases

---

[42] Starch became interested in this field from lectures which Walter Dill Scott delivered at the University of Iowa when Starch was a student there (Letter of January 13, 1954, from Daniel Starch).

[43] For a fuller discussion, see pp. 270–73 in *Principles of Advertising* (1923) by Daniel Starch.

by men and women. Omitting articles not purchased, the results showed that men bought 14 percent of the articles; women, 58 percent; and the two together, 28 percent.[132]

Starch also discussed the cost of advertising, largely from figures of cost to individual companies. He showed that people (businessmen, women, and men students), overestimated the expenditure for advertising of consumer goods by 4.5 times. He gave the results of advertising on sales and profits of individual companies and concluded that advertising can help reduce seasonal fluctuations in sales; that it promotes standardization and helps raise the quality of goods; that it has increased readership of newspapers and magazines by bearing much of the expense of their publication; that it raises the level of living by introducing new products, such as phonographs, vacuum cleaners, automobiles, and better houses and clothes; and that it "stimulates to a certain extent, perhaps a considerable extent, the actual total demand" by arousing desire among consumers for better things. Starch found no evidence that advertising increased the cost of distribution or raised prices to consumers.[132]

CHAPTER IV

Contributions, 1925–1939

Up to 1925 any new book in the field of marketing was received with interest, but after 1930 books on the subject became so numerous that one had to be really good to attract attention.

During the period 1925–1939, much factual information was secured. First should be listed the Census of Distribution for 1929, which presented a great mass of statistical information for analysis; it made possible, for example, estimates of the total cost of marketing of goods. Second in importance were the reports by the Federal Trade Commission on their investigation of chain stores and other subjects; and, third, the Department of Commerce's reports on the Louisville Grocery Survey, the St. Louis Drug Survey, and various studies of wholesale distribution costs.[1]

Various studies on the expenses and profits of retailers and wholesalers were published by the research bureaus of several universities, and by trade associations and business periodicals, especially in the years 1915 to 1930. The data indicated that the expenses of retailers increased with the volume of sales and with the size of towns in which the stores were located. In the mid-1930's, Dun & Bradstreet gathered enough reports to allow them to be broken down both by town size and by volume of sales. The data indicated that town size had a greater influence on the percentage of expense than did the volume of sales.

During the 1920's, questionnaire surveys came into wide use. To many laymen, the terms "marketing research" and "consumer surveys" were synonymous during much of the 1920's and 1930's.

Another valuable source of information to sellers was the Nielsen

[1] For a somewhat fuller discussion on contributions to the theory of marketing, see the article by Paul D. Converse, "Development of Marketing Theory; Fifty Years of Progress," in *Changing Perspectives in Marketing* (Hugh G. Wales, ed., University of Illinois Press, 1951), pp. 1–31.

indexes of retail food and drug sales started in 1933 by A. C. Nielsen. Somewhat later came the consumer panels which, with the use of diaries, gave valuable information of a somewhat similar type.

Notable Studies

Four studies which were of special importance during this period from 1925–1939 have been selected for comment.

Since the automobile was making trade much more mobile than it had been in the horse-and-buggy days, many marketing students were conducting research to ascertain how retail trade moved and the influence of the automobile and paved roads on its movements. Among these was William J. Reilly at The University of Texas, who in 1929 formulated his "law of retail gravitation." This law stated that towns attracted trade directly in proportion to their population and inversely as the squares of the distances to competitive territory.[138]

Many in the marketing field welcomed a mathematical formula which helped to make specific the general information on the subject of trade movements. Reilly's law stimulated thinking and promoted the gathering of specific information on the places where consumers purchased various kinds of goods and why they purchased them at these places.

Several other formulas derived from Reilly's formula or developed from the basic idea[2] have been of more practical use than Reilly's formula itself. It is now possible to predict where people trade and to define the trade areas of towns without actually making surveys. Some people think of a "science" as enabling students to make mathematical predictions. In this sense, Reilly's work has helped to make marketing "scientific."

The Brookings Institution published several studies dealing with America's capacity to produce and to consume.[3] The main thesis

[2] These formulas are summarized on pp. 746–50 in the 6th ed. of *Elements of Marketing* by Paul D. Converse, W. H. Huegy, and Robert V. Mitchell.

[3] Harold G. Moulton and Associates, *Income and Economic Progress* (1935); Edwin G. Nourse and Horace B. Drury, *Industrial Price Policies and Economic Progress* (1938); Edwin G. Nourse and Associates, *America's Ca-*

of these studies was that, as output per worker increases, prices should be reduced so that everyone can benefit. If output per worker increases 2 or 3 percent per year, then prices should be reduced 2 to 3 percent a year. It was argued that a bigger and bigger pie should be baked so that all could have more pie, rather than arguing over how the pie should be divided.

Another notable study was *High-Level Consumption* (1935) by William H. Lough and Martin R. Gainsbrugh. The authors point out that family income had been increasing, and predicted that if the rate of increase were maintained, the average family income would be equal to $2500 of 1913 dollars by the late 1940's. However, this income was not realized in the 1940's nor in the first half of the 1950's, probably because of the long and severe depression of the 1930's and the high taxes resulting from World War II.

Figures were also presented showing a slight decline in the cost of moving goods through wholesalers and retailers from 1909 to 1931 (from 35.5 to 33.3 percent of retail values). An explanation suggested was that the consumers were spending a larger portion of their income for large articles, such as automobiles, which required fewer man-hours to sell in relation to dollar values.

High-Level Consumption further pointed out that as family income increases, it becomes harder to predict how the family will spend its money.[4] When the family has some income left after the purchase of necessities, this surplus has come to be called "discretionary" buying power. To meet this uncertainty, Lough and Gainsbrugh said that two aspects were needed: (1) a new type of business executive who was market-minded and research-minded, and (2) smaller business enterprises which they felt could adjust more quickly to changes in demand.

The new type of business executive who is market-minded and research-minded has developed, but not the smaller business enterprises, perhaps because the development of market research enables large companies to adjust quickly to changes in demand. In fact, the large company can often employ more and better research

---

pacity to Produce (1934); and Maurice Levin, Harold G. Moulton, and Clark Warburton, *America's Capacity to Consume* (1934).

[4] See discussion of David A. Wells in Chapter I.

men than the small company and hence may be able to forecast demand better than can a small company with fewer or less competent researchers.

A fourth study that attracted wide attention, *Does Distribution Cost Too Much?*, was published in 1939 by the Twentieth Century Fund and authored by Paul W. Stewart, J. Frederick Dewhurst, and Louise Field. The title of the book is arresting, and it was widely read and quoted by marketing students and businessmen. Perhaps its main value was in assembling and publishing in one source much of the scattered data relating to the distribution of goods. One valuable contribution was the construction of a chart showing the flow of goods through the channels of distribution. The available data allowed the construction of a more accurate chart than was possible by Atkinson[5] thirty-seven years earlier.

A basic assumption of this volume was that distribution costs had been increasing, a conclusion not supported by their evidence. They ignored the study by Lough and Gainsbrugh which showed a slight decrease in moving goods through wholesalers and retailers from 1909 to 1931.[6] Later studies have shown little, if any, increase since 1869 and a slight decrease since 1929.[7]

The authors answer their own question, "Does distribution cost too much?" with "yes" because their research findings showed (1) opportunities for saving by reducing duplication of sales outlets, excessive services, multitudes of brands, unnecessary advertising,

[5] See discussion of Edward Atkinson in Chapter I.

[6] This conclusion seems to have been based on general opinion and partly on an index of efficiency of workers in distribution which they had constructed showing an increase of only 4 percent from 1870 to 1930 in contrast with 235 percent in production. They used only one index of the volume of production. Prior to the publication of this report, I had experimented with five indexes of physical production and had come up with a "guess" of an increase in output per worker in distribution of 77 percent from 1869 to 1929. If *Does Distribution Cost Too Much?* had, for example, used the *Standard Statistics Index* they would have shown that the output per worker in distribution more than doubled between 1889 and 1929 instead of their figure of an 11 percent increase. See *Journal of Marketing* (April 1940), pp. 424–27.

[7] The information is summarized on pp. 742–45 in the 6th edition of *Elements of Marketing* by Converse, Huegy, and Mitchell.

unreasonable demands and misinformed buying by consumers, and lack of knowledge and too much zeal for volume among distributors; and (2) some newer types of distributors showing economies in operation. "Taking the field of distribution as a whole the process undoubtedly costs too much. But how much too much is impossible to say."[134]

To attain better distribution, the authors recommended (a) more consumer knowledge including informative labeling, retail prices based on differences in services rendered, government testing, development of consumer cooperatives, and consumer education in schools; (b) more operating information and better performance by distributors; and (c) adherence to competitive system by repeal of any laws designed to destroy or preserve any special group of distributors, strengthening of laws and administration to prevent and destroy private monopoly, and repeal of state laws discriminating against products of other states.[134]

Summary of References*

1. Adams, Edward Francis. *The Modern Farmer in His Business Relations.* San Francisco, California: N. S. Stone Co., 1899.
2. Alderson, Wroe. "Biography on Charles Coolidge Parlin," *Journal of Marketing*, XXI, No. 1 (July 1956), pp. 1–2.
3. Archibald, J. P. As quoted in Paul T. Cherington, *Advertising as a Business Force*, p. 385.
4. Atkinson, Edward. *The Distribution of Products.* New York & London: G. P. Putnam's Sons, 1885.
5. Atkinson, Edward. *The Industrial Progress of the Nation.* New York & London: G. P. Putnam's Sons, 1889.
6. Atkinson, Edward. *Taxation and Work.* New York: G. P. Putnam's Sons, 1892.
7. Bates, Charles Austin. *Good Advertising.* New York: Holmes Publishing Co., 1896.
8. Benner, Samuel. *Benner's Prophecies of the Future Ups and Downs of Prices; What Years to Make Money on Pig-Iron, Hogs, Corn, Provisions.* 16th ed. Cincinnati: Robert Clarke Co., 1907. Subsequent eds.: 1st, 1876 (Cincinnati: the author). Others: 3d, 1884; 4th, 1888; 11th, 1897; 14th, 1904; 15th 1905 (Cincinnati: Robert Clarke Co.).
9. *Bradstreet's*, March 3, 1888.
10. Butler, Ralph Starr. *Marketing Methods.* New York: Alexander Hamilton Institute, 1917.
11. Butler, Ralph Starr. *Sales, Purchase, and Shipping Methods.* Madison: University of Wisconsin Extension Division, 1911.
12. Calkins, Earnest Elmo. *Business the Civilizer.* Boston: Little, Brown & Co., 1926.
13. Calkins, Earnest Elmo. *The Business of Advertising.* New York & London: D. Appleton & Co., 1915.

---

* Two kinds of references are included: (1) specific books or articles for which the earliest available date is given, and (2) supplementary references to illustrate the scope of the scholar's writing. In no case has a complete bibliography been attempted.

14. Calkins, Earnest Elmo, and Holden, Ralph. *Modern Advertising.* New York: D. Appleton & Co., 1905.
15. Chase, Stuart, and Schlink, F. J. *Your Money's Worth.* New York: The Macmillan Co., 1927.
16. Cherington, Paul T. *Advertising as a Business Force.* New York: Doubleday, Page & Co., 1913.
17. Cherington, Paul T. *The Elements of Marketing.* New York: The Macmillan Co., 1920.
18. Cherington, Paul T. *People's Wants and How to Satisfy Them.* New York: Harper & Bros., 1935.
19. Cherington, Paul T. *The Wool Industry.* Chicago: A. W. Shaw Co., 1916.
20. Clark, Fred E. "An Appraisal of Certain Criticisms of Advertising," *American Economic Review,* XV, No. 1, Supplement (March 1925), pp. 5–13.
21. Clark, Fred E. "Discussion of Weld's Paper on 'Do Principles of Large-Scale Production Apply to Merchandising?'," *American Economic Review,* XIII, No. 1, Supplement (March 1923), pp. 219–22.
22. Clark, Fred E. *Principles of Marketing.* New York: The Macmillan Co., 1922.
23. Clark, Fred E. *Readings in Marketing.* Revised. New York: The Macmillan Co., 1924, 1933.
24. Clark, Fred E., and Weld, L. D. H. *Marketing Agricultural Products in the United States.* New York: The Macmillan Co., 1932.
25. Colwell, Stephen. *The Ways and Means of Payment.* Philadelphia: J. B. Lippincott & Co., 1859.
26. Converse, Paul D. "Development of Marketing Theory; Fifty Years of Progress," in *Changing Perspectives in Marketing,* edited by Hugh G. Wales. Champaign: University of Illinois Press, 1951, pp. 1–31.
27. Converse, Paul D. "The Development of the Science of Marketing—An Exploratory Survey," *Journal of Marketing,* X, No. 1 (July 1945), pp. 14–23.
28. Converse, Paul D. "Fred Clark's Bibliography as of the Early 1920's," *Journal of Marketing,* X, No. 1 (July 1945), pp. 54–57.
29. Converse, Paul D. *Marketing Methods and Policies.* New York: Prentice-Hall, Inc., 1921; revised, enlarged, 1924.
30. Converse, Paul D. *Elements of Marketing.* New York: Prentice-

Hall, Inc., 1930; revised, 1935; with Harvey W. Huegy, 1940, 1946; with Harvey W. Huegy and Robert V. Mitchell, 1952, 1958.

31. Coolsen, Frank. "The Development of Systematic Instruction in the Principles of Advertising." Unpublished M.A. thesis (University of Illinois), 1942.
32. Coolsen, Frank. *Marketing Ideas of Selected Empirical Economists, 1870 to 1900*. Ph.D. thesis (University of Illinois), 1958.
33. Coolsen, Frank. "Pioneers in the Development of Advertising," *Journal of Marketing*, XII, No. 1 (July 1947), pp. 80–86.
34. Copeland, Melvin T. *The Cotton Manufacturing Industry of the United States*. Cambridge, Massachusetts: Harvard University Press, 1912.
35. Copeland, Melvin T. *Marketing Problems*. Chicago: A. W. Shaw Co., 1920.
36. Copeland, Melvin T. *Principles of Merchandising*. Chicago: A. W. Shaw Co., 1924.
37. Copeland, Melvin T. "Relation of Consumer Buying Habits to Marketing Methods," *Harvard Business Review*, I (April 1923), pp. 282–89.
38. Douglas, Archer Wall. *Merchandising*. New York: The Macmillan Co., 1918.
39. Duncan, C. S. *Commercial Research*. New York: The Macmillan Co., 1919.
40. Duncan, C. S. *Marketing: Its Problems and Methods*. New York: D. Appleton & Co., 1920.
41. Emerson, Ralph Waldo. "Works and Days" (Essay), in *Society and Solitude*. Boston: Field, Osgood & Co., 1870. [Also, Boston & New York: Houghton Mifflin Co., 1903–04.]
42. Emery, Henry C. *Company Management;* a Manual for the Daily Use of Directors, Secretaries and Others, in the Formation and Management of Joint Stock Companies under the Companies Act. 2d ed. revised, 1912. London: E. Wilson, revised by R. Borregard, 1930.
43. Emery, Henry C. *Speculation on the Stock and Produce Exchanges of the United States*. Columbia University Studies in History, Economics, and Public Law, VII, No. 2 (1896).
44. Farquhar, Arthur. "My Sixty-Four Years in Business" (a series of articles), *System*. Chicago: A. W. Shaw Co., 1920–21: (August 1920), pp. 232–35, 286, 289, 290; (September 1920), pp. 411–13, 546; (October 1920), pp. 626–28, 738, 741, 742, 744, 747, 749;

(November 1920), pp. 836–38, 902, 905, 906, 908, 910, 912; (December 1920), pp. 1050–52, 1100, 1102, 1106, 1108, 1110; (January 1921), pp. 29–32, 108, 109, 110, 111; (February 1921), pp. 200–02, 232, 235, 236; (March 1921), pp. 385–87, 477, 478, 479; (April 1921), p. 521; also (May 1921), (June 1921), and (July 1921).

45. Farquhar, Arthur B., and Crowther, Samuel. *The First Million the Hardest.* Garden City, New York: Doubleday, Page & Co., 1922.
46. Farquhar, Arthur B., and Farquhar, Henry. *Economic and Industrial Delusions.* New York: G. P. Putnam's Sons, 1891.
47. Federal Trade Commission. *Bakery Combines and Profits* (Report). Doc. 212, 69th Cong., Vol. 22, 8713. Washington, D.C.: Government Printing Office, 1927. W. H. S. Stevens.
48. Federal Trade Commission. *Canned Foods;* General Report and Fruits and Vegetables (Report). Washington, D.C.: Government Printing Office, 1918–19. Kemper Simpson and Paul D. Converse.
49. Federal Trade Commission. *Causes of High Prices of Farm Implements* (Report). Washington, D.C.: Government Printing Office, May 4, 1920. Paul D. Converse.
50. Federal Trade Commission. *Furniture* (Report). Washington, D.C.: Government Printing Office, January 17, 1923. W. H. S. Stevens and Walter Durand.
51. Federal Trade Commission. *Investigation of Chain Stores* (Report). 34 reports published as Sen. Docs. from December 1931 to December 1934: 72d Cong., 1st Sess., 12, 29, 30, 31, 51, 82, 100; 72d Cong., 2d Sess., 130, 142, 153, 156, 170, 178; 73d Cong., 1st Sess., 13, 40, 62, 69, 84; 73d Cong., 2d Sess., 81, 82, 85, 86, 87, 88, 89, 91, 93, 94, 95, 96, 97, 98, 99; 74th Cong., 1st Sess., 4. W. H. S. Stevens.
52. Federal Trade Commission. *Report on the Grain Trade* (Report). Vols. 1, 2, & 5, September 15, 1920. Washington, D.C.: Government Printing Office, June 25, 1926. W. H. S. Stevens, and Others.
53. Fisk, George Mygatt. *International Commercial Policies.* New York: The Macmillan Co., 1907.
54. Foster, B. V. *The Merchant's Manual;* a Concise Treatise on Bookkeeping; Elucidating the Principles and Practice of Double Entry and the Modern Methods of Arranging Merchants' Accounts. Boston: Perkins, 1937.

55. Fowler, Nathaniel C. *Building Business*. Boston: The Trade Co., 1892.
56. Fowler, Nathaniel C. *Publicity*. New York: Publicity Publishing Co., 1897.
57. Frederick, J. George. *Business Research and Statistics*. New York: D. Appleton-Century Co., 1920.
58. Frederick, J. George. *Masters of Advertising Copy, Principles and Practice*. New York: Frank-Maurice, Inc., 1925. Also, The Business Bourse, 1936.
59. Frederick, J. George. *Modern Sales Management*. New York: D. Appleton & Co., 1919.
60. Frederick, J. George. *Modern Salesmanship*. Garden City, New York: Garden City Publishing Co., Inc., 1925.
61. Frederick, J. George. *A Philosophy of Production*. New York: The Business Bourse, 1930.
62. Frederick, J. George. *Selling by Telephone*. New York: The Business Bourse, 1928.
63. Freedley, E. T. *A Practical Treatise on Business*. Philadelphia: Lippincott, Grambo & Co., 1852.
64. Gage, Raymond W. *Printers' Ink*, LXXII, No. 6 (August 1910), pp. 8–13, as quoted in Paul T. Cherington, *Advertising as a Business Force*, p. 33.
65. Gale, Harlow. "On the Psychology of Advertising," *Psychological Studies* (Pamphlet). Minneapolis: the author, July 1900.
66. Galloway, Lee. *Office Management; Its Principles and Practice; Covering Organization, Arrangement and Operation*. New York: The Ronald Press Co., 1918.
67. Greene, Asa. *The Perils of Pearl Street*. New York: Betts & Anstice, and Peter Hill, 1834.
68. Hadley, A. T. *Railroad Transportation, Its History and Laws*. New York & London: G. P. Putnam's Sons, 1885.
69. Hagerty, J. E. "Experiences of an Early Marketing Teacher," *Journal of Marketing*, I, No. 1, (July 1936), pp. 20–27.
70. Hall, S. Roland. *The Advertising Handbook*. New York: McGraw-Hill Book Co., Inc., 1921; 2d ed., 1930.
71. Hall, S. Roland. *Business Writing*. New York: McGraw-Hill Book Co., Inc., 1923.
72. Hall, S. Roland. *The Fundamentals of Advertising Campaigns*. Scranton, Pennsylvania: International Correspondence Schools, 1935. Serial No. 2101-2, Ed. 1.

73. Hall, S. Roland. *The Handbook of Sales Management.* New York: McGraw-Hill Book Co., Inc., 1924.
74. Hall, S. Roland. *Mail-Order and Direct-Mail Selling.* New York: McGraw-Hill Book Co., Inc., 1928.
75. Hall, S. Roland. *Retail Advertising and Selling.* New York: McGraw-Hill Book Co., Inc., 1924.
76. Hall, S. Roland. *Theory and Practice of Advertising.* New York: McGraw-Hill Book Co., Inc., 1926.
77. Hall, S. Roland. *Writing an Advertisement;* an Analysis of the Methods and Mental Processes that Play an Important Part in Writing Successful Advertising. Boston: Houghton Mifflin Co., 1915.
78. Huebner, Grover C. *Agricultural Commerce.* New York: D. Appleton & Co., 1915; revised, 1924.
79. Hunt, Freeman H. *Lives of American Merchants.* New York: Derby & Jackson; Cincinnati: H. W. Derby & Co., 1858.
80. *Hunt's Magazine,* XV, p. 475, as quoted in Paul Nystrom, *Economics of Retailing,* pp. 301–02.
81. Johnson, Emory R. *American Railroad Transportation.* New York: D. Appleton & Co., 1903, 1907, 1912.
82. Lardner, Dionysius. *Railway Economy.* London: Taylor, Walton & Maberly, 1850.
83. Levin, Maurice; Moulton, Harold G.; and Warburton, Clark. *America's Capacity to Consume.* Washington, D.C.: The Brookings Institution, 1934.
84. Litman, Simon. "The Beginnings of Teaching Marketing in American Universities," *Journal of Marketing,* XV, No. 2 (October 1950), pp. 220–23.
85. Lough, William H., and Gainsbrugh, Martin R. *High-Level Consumption; Its Behavior; Its Consequences.* New York & London: McGraw-Hill Book Co., Inc., 1935.
86. Moriarty, W. D. *Economics of Marketing and Advertising.* New York & London: Harper & Bros., 1923.
87. Moulton, Harold G., and Associates. *Income and Economic Progress.* Washington, D.C.: The Brookings Institution, 1935.
88. *Nation,* April 12, 1888, as quoted in Paul Nystrom, *Economics of Retailing,* pp. 301–02.
89. National Cash Register Co. *The Primer.* Dayton, Ohio: The National Cash Register Co., 1894.

90. Newcomb, Harry Turner. *Railway Economics.* Philadelphia: Railway World Publishing Co., 1898.
91. Nourse, Edwin G., and Associates. *America's Capacity to Produce.* Washington, D.C.: The Brookings Institution, 1934.
92. Nourse, Edwin G., and Drury, Horace B. *Industrial Price Policies and Economic Progress.* Washington, D.C.: The Brookings Institution, 1938.
93. Nystrom, Paul. *Economics of Fashion.* New York: The Ronald Press Co., 1928.
94. Nystrom, Paul. *Economics of Retailing.* New York: The Ronald Press Co., 1915.
95. Nystrom, Paul. *Fashion Merchandising.* New York: The Ronald Press Co., 1932.
96. Parlin, Charles Coolidge. *History of the Curtis Commercial Research Department.* Philadelphia: Curtis Publishing Co. (Speech, June 5, 1936).
97. Parlin, Charles Coolidge. *The Merchandising of Automobiles* (Pamphlet). Philadelphia: The Curtis Publishing Co., 1915.
98. Parlin, Charles Coolidge. *The Merchandising of Textiles* (Pamphlet). Philadelphia: The Curtis Publishing Co., 1915.
99. Parlin, Charles Coolidge. *Selling Forces* (Pamphlet). Philadelphia: The Curtis Publishing Co., 1913.
100. Russell, Frederick A. *The Management of the Sales Organization.* New York: McGraw-Hill Book Co., Inc., 1922.
101. Russell, Frederick A. *Textbook of Salesmanship.* New York & London: McGraw-Hill Book Co., Inc., 1924; 3d ed., 1941, with Frank Herman Beach; 5th ed., 1955, with Frank Herman Beach.
102. Sammons, Wheeler. *How to Run a Retail Business at Greater Profit.* Chicago & New York: A. W. Shaw Co., 1915; 4th ed., 1919. Also published in 1915 as *Keeping Up With Rising Costs.*
103. Sammons, Wheeler. *Keeping Up With Rising Costs.* New York & Chicago: A. W. Shaw Co., 1915.
104. Sammons, Wheeler. "Keeping Up With Rising Costs," *System Magazine* (1915).
105. Sammons, Wheeler (ed.). *Making More Out of Advertising.* Chicago: A. W. Shaw Co., 1919.
106. Schultz, Henry. *The Theory and Measurement of Demand.* Chicago: University of Chicago Press, 1938.
107. Scott, Walter Dill. *Increasing Human Efficiency in Business.* New York: The Macmillan Co., 1911, 1912.

108. Scott, Walter Dill. *Influencing Men in Business*. New York: The Ronald Press Co., 1911, 1919, 1928.
109. Scott, Walter Dill. "Psychology of Advertising," *Atlantic Monthly*, XCIII, No. DLV (January 1904), pp. 29–36.
110. Scott, Walter Dill. *The Psychology of Advertising*. Boston: Small, Maynard & Co., 1908, 1910, 1912, 1921. New York: Dodd, Mead & Co., revised, 1931.
111. Scott, Walter Dill. *The Psychology of Public Speaking*. Philadelphia: Pearson Bros., 1907. New York: Noble & Noble, revised, 1926.
112. Scott, Walter Dill. *The Theory of Advertising*. Boston: Small, Maynard & Co., 1903.
113. Scott, Walter Dill, and Clothier, Robert C. *Personnel Management*. Chicago & New York: A. W. Shaw Co., 1923, 1925, 1931, 1941, 1949; 3d ed. with Stanley B. Mathewson and William R. Spriegel.
114. Scott, Walter Dill, and Hayes, M. H. S. *Science and Common Sense in Working with Men*. New York: The Ronald Press Co., 1921.
115. Scoville, J. A. (under the pseudonym "Walter Barrett, Clerk"). *The Old Merchants of New York City*. New York: Carleton, 1863.
116. Secrist, Horace. *A Business Barometer for Retailers* (Bulletin). Chicago: Northwestern University Business Research Bureau, 1922.
117. Secrist, Horace. *Commercial Rent as an Expense and Its Relation to Profits* (Bulletin). Chicago: Northwestern University Business Research Bureau, 1923.
118. Secrist, Horace. *Competition in the Retail Distribution of Clothing* (Bulletin). Chicago: Northwestern University Business Research Bureau, 1923.
119. Secrist, Horace. *Cost, Merchandising Practices, Advertising, and Sales in Retail Distribution of Clothing*, 5 vols. New York: Prentice-Hall, Inc., 1921.
120. Secrist, Horace. *Expense, Profits, and Losses in Retail Meat Stores* (Bulletin). Chicago: Northwestern University Business Research Bureau, 1924.
121. Secrist, Horace. *Expense Levels in Retailing—A Study of the Representative Firm and of Bulk Line Costs in Distribution of Clothing* (Bulletin). Chicago: Northwestern University Business Research Bureau, 1924.

122. Secrist, Horace. *Introduction to Statistical Methods.* New York: The Macmillan Co., 1917; revised, 1925.
123. Secrist, Horace. *Margins, Expenses, and Profits of Retail Hardware Stores* (Bulletin). Chicago & New York: A. W. Shaw Co., 1928. London: A. W. Shaw & Co., Ltd., 1928.
124. Secrist, Horace. *A Seven Year View of Sales and Expenses of Retail Clothiers 1916 to 1922* (Bulletin). Chicago: Northwestern University Business Research Bureau, 1924.
125. Secrist, Horace. *Stockturnover in Retail Clothing Stores* (Bulletin). Chicago: Northwestern University Business Research Bureau, 1922.
126. Secrist, Horace. *The Triumph of Mediocrity.* Evanston, Illinois: Northwestern University Business Research Bureau, 1933.
127. Secrist, Horace. *The Widening Retail Market and Buying Habits* (Bulletin). Chicago & New York: A. W. Shaw Co.; London: A. W. Shaw & Co., Ltd., 1926.
128. Shaw, Arch W. *An Approach to Business Problems.* Cambridge, Massachusetts: Harvard University Press, 1916.
129. Shaw, Arch W. *Some Problems in Market Distribution.* Cambridge, Massachusetts: Harvard University Press, 1915.
130. Shaw, Arch W. "Some Problems in Market Distribution," *Quarterly Journal of Economics,* XXVI (August 1912), pp. 703–65. Revised and expanded into book form in 1915.
131. Starch, Daniel. *Advertising: Its Principles, Practice, and Techniques.* Chicago & New York: Scott, Foresman & Co., 1914.
132. Starch, Daniel. *Principles of Advertising.* Chicago & New York: A. W. Shaw Co., 1923.
133. Stevens, W. H. S. *Unfair Competition.* Chicago: University of Chicago Press, 1917.
134. Stewart, Paul W.; Dewhurst, J. Frederick; and Field, Louise. *Does Distribution Cost Too Much?* New York: Twentieth Century Fund, 1939.
135. Stocking, Collis A. "Modern Advertising and Economic Theory," *American Economic Review,* XXI, No. 1 (March 1931), pp. 43–55.
136. Tarbell, Ida M. *The History of the Standard Oil Company.* New York: McClure Phillips & Co., 1904; reprinted in 1950 by P. Smith.
137. Terry, Samuel H. *The Retailer's Manual or How to Keep a Store.* 16 eds. issued. Newark: Jennings Bros., 1869; also, New York: Fowler & Wells, 1882.

138. The University of Texas, Bureau of Business Research. *Methods for the Study of Retail Relationships*. Mon. No. 4. Austin, Texas: Bureau of Business Research, The University of Texas, 1929.
139. U.S. Bureau of Corporations. *Report of the Commissioner of Corporations on the Beef Industry* (Report). Washington, D.C.: Government Printing Office, March 3, 1905.
140. U.S. Bureau of Corporations. *Report of the Commissioner of Corporations on the Cotton Exchanges* (Report). Washington, D.C.: Government Printing Office, 1908–09.
141. U.S. Bureau of Corporations. *Report of the Commissioner of Corporations on the Lumber Industry* (Summary). Washington, D.C.: Government Printing Office, 1911.
142. U.S. Bureau of Corporations. *Report of the Commissioner of Corporations on the Petroleum Industry* (Report). Washington, D.C.: Government Printing Office, 1907.
143. U.S. Bureau of Corporations. *Report of the Commissioner of Corporations, on the Steel Industry* (Report). Washington, D. C.: Government Printing Office, 1911–13.
144. U.S. Bureau of Corporations. *Report of the Commissioner of Corporations on the Tobacco Industry* (Report). Washington, D.C.: Government Printing Office, 1909.
145. U.S. Bureau of Corporations. *Report of the Commissioner of Corporations on the Transportation of Petroleum* (Report). Washington, D.C.: Government Printing Office, 1906.
146. U.S. Bureau of Corporations. *Report of the Commissioner of Corporations on Transportation by Water* (Report). Washington, D.C.: Government Printing Office, 1909–13.
147. U.S. Chamber of Commerce [Chamber of Commerce of the United States of America]. *Relations of Weather and Business* (2 pamphlets). 1919.
148. U.S. Department of Agriculture, Weather Bureau; Douglas, Archer Wall. "Relations of Weather and Business," *Monthly Weather Review*, XLVII, No. 12 (December 1919), p. 867.
149. U.S. Industrial Commission. *Report on the Distribution of Farm Products*, 19 vols. Vol. VI: "Reports of the Industrial Commission." Washington, D. C.: Government Printing Office, 1900–02.
150. Van Hise, Charles R. *Concentration and Control*. New York: The Macmillan Co., 1912.
151. Weld, L. D. H. "Marketing Agencies Between Manufacturer and

Studies in Marketing No. 5

Fifty Years of Marketing in Retrospect

BY

Paul D. Converse
Visiting Professor of Marketing
The University of Texas

BUREAU OF BUSINESS RESEARCH
THE UNIVERSITY OF TEXAS, AUSTIN : 1959

Foreword

The Bureau of Business Research is pleased to have the opportunity to publish FIFTY YEARS OF MARKETING IN RETROSPECT as Studies in Marketing No. 5 because the staff believes that Dr. Converse's informal reminiscences of the development of marketing will prove to be of wide interest to those associated with the field. This bulletin is a companion study to THE BEGINNING OF MARKETING THOUGHT IN THE UNITED STATES (Studies in Marketing No. 3) which Dr. Converse wrote and which the Bureau published earlier this year.

To many the name of Paul D. Converse is almost synonymous with the word marketing. He not only is an outstanding teacher of the vital area of marketing and distribution, but he has also been a shrewd and interested scholar of those subjects since he was a small boy. Those of us on the faculty of the College of Business Administration of The University of Texas and the students in Dr. Converse's classes while he was a visiting professor here are grateful for the privilege of having had the opportunity to work with him. His lively and shrewd observations and his delightful sense of humor inspired all who came in contact with him.

Mrs. Elizabeth R. Turpin edited the manuscript for publication.

STANLEY A. ARBINGAST
Assistant Director

October 1959

Preface

I recall learning in geology that there have been long periods with little change in the forms of life; then in relatively short periods great changes took place. So it has been in the history of men. There have been long periods when life went along with little change; then relatively short periods great changes were made. We think of the few centuries of Greek history when learning, philosophy, literature, art, and architecture developed and flourished; of the developments of law and civilization in the last years of the Roman Republic and the early years of the Empire; and of those in Hebrew history—the rapid developments, political and economic, under kings David and Solomon.

The western world has seen many and rapid changes in education, economics, and government since the Renaissance and the Protestant Reformation. Yet during these centuries the rate of change (often called "progress") has varied greatly. The greatest changes in our economic life have come since the invention of the steam engine—which made possible large factories, steamships, and railroads—and the electric dynamo. In the United States economic progress has been especially rapid since the building of the railroads and the development of factories in the last thirty or forty years of the nineteenth century. One writer in 1889 said:

The wonderful material progress which has been made within the past quarter of a century has probably done more to overcome the inertia and quicken the energy of the masses than has been hereto achieved in this direction in all preceding centuries. . . . The [masses] have come to know more of what others are doing; know better what they are capable of doing; and their wants have correspondingly increased, and not merely in respect to quantities of the things to which they have always been accustomed, but very many articles and services which within a comparatively recent period were regarded as luxuries, are now almost universally considered and demanded as necessities.*

* David A. Wells, *Recent Economic Changes* (New York: D. Appleton & Co., 1889).

The railroads not only speeded up deliveries but reduced costs. Edward Atkinson[*] estimated that the freight cost on all commodities brought to New York by rail decreased from 36.6 percent of their value in New York in 1869 to 17.9 percent in 1883. The reduced cost and increased speed enabled producers to secure large markets which in turn made large-scale production possible.

The economic progress during the years is shown by the increase in *real* per capita income of 103 percent in the thirty years from 1911 to 1941 and an increase in per capita real disposable income of 57 percent in the twenty-eight years from 1929 to 1957. Taxes are much higher now than they were prior to 1940 and materially reduce disposable income. The consumers, of course, receive certain benefits from the higher taxes in highways, schools, hospitals, health protection, research, playgrounds, and parks. Nevertheless, if the statistics are even approximately correct, our economic well being has improved much more slowly since 1920 than during the preceding fifty years.

In the 1890's many felt that we had found out about all that there was to know. Then the X-ray was discovered and the decomposition of radium observed. These showed that we really knew very little about the nature of matter and started us on a new era of scientific investigation.

PAUL D. CONVERSE

1959

[*] Edward Atkinson, *Distribution of Products* (New York & London: G. P. Putnam's Sons, 1885).

Table of Contents

	PAGE
Foreword	iii
Preface	v
Introduction	xi

CHAPTER

I. From "Drummers" to Gadgets 1
    Wholesalers and "Drummers" 2
    Business Recovery from the Depression of
        the 1890's 4
    Rise of Advertising 5

II. 1900–1917–High Cost of Living Era 7
    Rise of Living Costs 7
    Wholesaling 8
    Retailing 9
    Mail-Order Houses and Chain Stores 9
    Railroading 10
    Growth of Central Power Stations 11
    Prohibition 12
    Increase in Education 12
    Pure Food Law 13
    Truth in Advertising 14
    Increased Consumption of Fruits and
        Vegetables 14
    Panic of 1907 15
    Prices of Farm Products 16
    New Industries 16
    Trust Movement 18
    Passing of the Barons 19
    Henry Ford and the Assembly Line 23
    Theory of High Wages 24

III. 1917–1921—World War I and the Ensuing
    Depression 25
    Wartime Controls 25
    Break in Prices 26
    Price Guarantees 28
    Recovery 28

IV. 1922–1929—New Industrial Revolution 30
    Increase in Output per Worker 30
    Research 32
    Prohibition 33
    Motor Age 34
    Growing Up of the Chain Store 37
    Competition by the Independent Retailers . . 40
    Farm Problem 41
    Stable Price Theory 42

V. The 1930's—Desire for Security 44
    Big Break, 1929–1932 44
    Administered Prices 48
    Consumer Movement 51
    Declining Birth Rate 53
    New Deal 53
    National Recovery Administration 55
    "Boondoggling" 56
    Farm Aid 57
    Other Programs 60
    Legislation Against Price Cutting 61
    Robinson-Patman Amendment 62
    Supermarkets 64
    Branch Stores 67
    Motor Truck Transportation 67
    Recession and Recovery 69
    Evaluation 70
    Economic Power and the Residual Theory . . . 72

VI. World War II 74
    Price Controls 75
    Postwar Inflation 76

VII. 1946–1959—Gadget Economy 77
    Population 77
    Income 79
    Income Classes 82
    Purchase of Gadgets 83
    Capital Expenditures 84
    Research 85
    Services 86
    Recession and Korea 86
    Inflationary Hypothesis 87
    Free Trade and World Aid 89
    Suburban Shopping Centers 91
    Offices in the Suburbs 92
    Movement of Factories to the Country . . . 93
    Increase in Self-Service 94
    Discount Selling 94
    Physical Handling 96
    Diversification and Mixed Lines 96
    Theory of the Gadget Economy, the 1950's . . 97

Conclusions 102

Introduction

This is the story of business and particularly of market distribution as I have seen it and as I have studied it. As one grows up he sees and remembers many things. The conditions he finds he takes to be the established and accepted methods of living and doing business. It is not until later when he talks to older people, reads books, or studies history that he finds that many of the devices and many of the methods of doing things which he accepted as long established were in reality relatively new.

Personally, I accepted the railroad, the electric light, the telegraph, the telephone, and artificial ice as well established. The local cobbler was a repairman and not a shoemaker. Men's suits, overcoats, shirts, underwear, and socks were factory made. However, women were still making many of their dresses, and their hats were usually trimmed by a local milliner. Most of the wagons were made by the local blacksmiths, but buggies were factory made. The automobile, the moving picture, the radio, the airplane, the domestic electrical refrigerator, the phonograph, the tabulating machine, vitamins, antibiotics, the television set, the air conditioners—all have been new things to me.

After I was six years old I was sent to a nearby town to buy many of the family groceries and so became familiar with the grocery stores. When I was older I often went with my father who was a country preacher. To pass the tedious time in traveling country roads by buggy I often watched the telephone lines to see which company covered which roads, and which farmers had telephones. I talked to the farmers about how many acres of corn and other crops they raised, how many bushels per acre they harvested, and how much farm laborers were paid (40 and 50 cents for a day of ten or twelve hours), and where they sold their products.

The traveling salesmen or "drummers" were very important. Many of the boys dropped out of school when they were 15 or 16 to become traveling salesmen after they learned the business by working as stock boys in a wholesale house for a few years. Many of them made good salesmen. I used to talk to the salesmen and ask them what they sold, where and how they traveled, and sometimes how much their sales amounted to. I learned the printer's trade and had to talk to the local merchants when I set their ads or did their job printing. The local newspaper office was somewhat of a clearing house for political and business information and the boy who kept his ears open and his mouth shut could learn a lot about what went on in the community. For example, I learned that very few of the merchants on Main Street were "making any money." Like most youngsters I had supposed that all the merchants made money. The distinction hinges on a meaning of *money*. I was surprised to hear that the merchant who operated the "Pound Store," selling cloth by the pound, was one of the few making money. He bought remnants and sold them by the pound. He claimed to do both a retail and wholesale business. As I recall, there were three wholesalers or jobbers in the town in 1900 while by 1907 there were nine wholesalers including two semijobbers of hardware but excluding the Pound Store. This was the period when local wholesalers were increasing rapidly.

There were twenty-odd retail grocers. Many of them were short-lived. Assignments and foreclosures were common but the same man often opened another store in a very short time. After a third wholesale grocery house was opened, competition was so keen that daily calls were made by salesmen on all these little grocery stores.

The railroad was the "big" thing and a common diversion was to go to the depot to see the trains come in or to watch the local freight switch cars. A story was that a stranger once asked our chief of police the population of the town. The chief looked up and down the platform and replied, "They are all here, just count them." The ambition of many of the boys was "to railroad" and to become engineers. Seniority was important, but some of the boys stuck to railroading until they got their engines. Some boys went into their fathers' businesses; some went back to the farms; and some went to clerking in the retail stores with the idea of having their own stores some day; and some went away to college to become lawyers, doctors, preachers, chemists, or professors. I came in the last class. I entered college in 1909, became an instructor in 1912, and began to teach transportation in 1913, foreign trade in 1914, and general marketing and management in the academic year 1915–1916.

This story is written very largely from memory, although I must confess that I have looked up a few figures.

CHAPTER I

From "Drummers" to Gadgets

The American economy of 1900 and that of 1959 are different in some ways but alike in others. In 1900 few people believed that they would ever ride in horseless carriages or fly through the air. However, 1900 was in an age of marvels. The railroads were built and passenger trains ran as fast as at any time prior to the 1930's; the telegraph, the telephone, the electric light, the electric motor, the electric streetcar were well-known modern inventions of which Americans were proud. Artificial ice was available in nearly all towns. The large department stores were the marvels of the large cities, and Sears Roebuck and Montgomery Ward and other mail-order catalogs were finding their way into rural homes. It is doubtful if the people of 1959 marvel as much over the automobile, airplane, radio, colored TV, atomic energy, diesel engines, digital computers, and antibiotics as did the people of 1900 over the railroad, the electric light, and the telephone.

There have nevertheless been great changes in the way in which people live. Machinery has greatly increased the output per man in factories, on farms, and in mines. Work hours are shorter. The national income has increased faster than prices and population, leading to considerably higher family incomes; and the income is more evenly distributed so that there is much less difference in the way people in different occupations and in different parts of the country live. The people of 1959 have many more gadgets—electric refrigerators, vacuum cleaners, radios, automatic washing machines and dryers, bath tubs, fur coats, frozen foods, flour mixes, precooked foods, automobiles, paved roads, air conditioners, TV's, colored pictures, and so on. In 1890 the physicists were sure that they knew all the answers to questions about the nature of matter. Then the X-ray was discovered and the disintegration of radium observed. These opened up an entirely new universe. However, in

1900 few if any people had even a glimmering of the significance of these discoveries.

My purpose is to trace the developments in the economy from 1900 to 1959 with especial reference to the ways in which goods are distributed. There has been a "miracle" of production. There has been an equally important "miracle" of distribution.

I will tell the story of changes in gadgets, in distribution methods, in the United States economy, and in the way people live as I have seen them.

Wholesalers and "Drummers"*

In 1900 the wholesaler was in his prime and the drummers were the proud symbol of American commerce. These drummers carried goods to the largest and smallest stores whether located in crowded metropolitan streets, in sequestered mountain valleys, or out on the windswept prairies. They gave the factories outlets for their goods and brought a variety of goods to the stores in the small towns and villages. It was much cheaper for the salesmen to visit the retailers than for each retailer to leave his store and visit markets in distant cities as had been the custom. The drummers became important with the growth of the railroads in the years following the Civil War and particularly in the 1870's and the 1880's. There were relatively few on the road prior to 1860.

The life and work of the drummers in the 1900's was interesting. They were among the leading patrons of the local passenger trains and some rode the caboose or the old passenger car attached to the local freight. They traveled the back country by hack, by

* The "drummer" originally was one who "drummed" up trade by meeting out of town buyers in the hotels, at the wharves, and later at railroad depots, becoming friendly with them and inducing them to visit his employer's place of business. The word "drum" came from one who attracted attention by beating a drum to get people to follow him. With the building of the railroads, the drummers went to the country to make friends with the merchants and to invite them to visit their stores when the merchants came to town. The drummers soon began taking orders and developed eventually into traveling salesmen. One estimate or guess (Edward P. Briggs, *Fifty Years on the Road* [Philadelphia: Lyon and Armor, 1911]) was that there were not more than one thousand traveling salesmen in the United States in 1861.

buggy, and on horseback. They very largely supported the small-town hotels which operated on the American plan at $2 a day—50 cents for a meal and 50 cents for a bed (by 1917 some had raised their prices to $3 or even $3.50). Many of these hotels served good food and some had good beds. In the large cities, however, the hotels operated on the European plan, usually charging from $1 to $2.50 per day for room. If in the small towns the hotels were several blocks from the depot, buses—often free—were usually operated to meet all trains. Meal times at these hotels were controlled by train schedules. If the morning train "ran" at seven o'clock, the hotel would serve breakfast in time for passengers to get the train. However, if the morning train was scheduled at five in the morning, the salesmen ate at their next stop down the line.

The drummers mastered this way of living. Many carried the minimum of personal belongings. Some could take the bellboy's call, dress, and catch the train across the street in fifteen or twenty minutes. Trains were often late, and information as to the time of their arrival was often lacking or inaccurate. The drummers took this with professional nonchalance while others stewed and fumed at the delays.

There were several types of drummers. Some of those selling apparel carried trunks full of samples. These trunks had to be taken by drays to the hotels where they were displayed in sample rooms, and, after they were shown to local merchants, repacked and returned to the depot. In a good trading center town several baggage trucks were often piled high with these trunks which got rough handling and not infrequently were dropped. The common joke was that in this way the railroads tested their platforms. If the falling trunks did not break the platform, it was made of sound materials. These drummers or salesmen usually made only the larger places such as the county seats and trading center towns, although some loaded their trunks in hacks and made the back country. They represented both wholesalers and manufacturers.

Perhaps the second type, which were probably more numerous, could be classed as jobbers' salesmen, many of whom carried only catalogs with perhaps a very few samples of specials which they were "pushing." They called on city, village, and rural merchants. They traveled by trains where there were trains. Where there were no trains they hired hacks, or buggies, or stuffed their catalogs in saddlepockets and rode horseback over roads too poor for vehicles. They might travel by buggy in summer and on horseback in winter. They began using automobiles before 1910, but the automobile did not take the place of the train until roads were improved in the 1920's. With the automobile the salesmen could make more calls per day, could spend more nights at home, and could drive into the larger towns where the hotel accommodations were better. This meant the village hotels were doomed and also that the rise of automobiles was hastened. The resulting situation also marked the demise of the local and branch-line passenger trains. Although the automobile has proved better for the salesman, one cannot avoid a little nostalgia for the sociability of the lobbies of the little hotels.

The third type of drummer—the specialty or "missionary" salesman—carried a very short line, often only one small item such as Easter egg dyes, or a small toilet article, or a grocery product. He often carried his samples in his pockets, and he usually made only the railroad towns. People often marveled how the sale of a single small item would justify the expenses of the salesmen. Likely most of them were used to introduce new products or to make occasional rounds to pep up lagging sales.

Business Recovery from the Depression of the 1890's

In 1900 the country was recovering from the very serious depression of the 1890's. Some few signs of recovery had appeared in 1895 and 1896. Some say that the election of 1896 with the defeat of Bryan and the proposal for free coinage of silver gave the country confidence and started recovery. Others say that the Spanish-American War in 1898 with the knowledge that America had become a world power gave the real impetus. Still others attribute the recovery to gold from the Klondike and some to industrialization and increased population of Western Europe with its demand for American farm products. An aiding factor was the low price of steel which encouraged the construction of industrial buildings and equipment. Probably it was a combination of all these and others.

The railroads were built. Electrc lights and artificial ice were widely used; telephones were coming into general use; rural free delivery routes were being established but parcel post was some years in the future. Electric streetcars were moving city people faster and spreading out the cities. The electric interurban railways were built in the years 1900–1904. Mail-order houses were small but mail-order selling was growing while wagon retailing was near its peak. The automobile was in the experimental stage although a few races had been run on city streets. The traveling repertoire company and the small-town opera house had grown with the railroad network in the 1870's. The traveling stock companies had their downfall, however, in the winter of 1907–1908, and the coming of movies and the depression combined to administer the knockout blow. In the winter of 1907–1908 there were said to be sixty-five or seventy stock companies stranded in Chicago.

Rise of Advertising

National advertising was becoming an important factor in business. Sales of packaged goods were growing. Arbuckle's roasted packaged coffee was placed on the market in 1865 by a wholesale grocer—Arbuckle Brothers. Although not the first packaged coffee, it was the first successful national brand of coffee. Arbuckle introduced premiums in 1895. When the Arbuckle Company entered sugar refining, the Haveymerer interests bought the Woolsen Company and started to fight Arbuckle with the Lion brand of roasted coffee.* I recall seeing Lion brand coffee in the grocery store window in the middle 1890's at 8¢ a pound. According to my memory the common price of Arbuckle coffee was around 16¢ although it was undoubtedly less during this price war.

The peddler with his pack of cloth, tin ware, and clocks carried on his back or in wagons had passed from the scene. He had been

* William H. Ukers, *Nation's Business*, July 1923.

largely replaced by the general store. In the 1900's the specialty store was replacing the general store. The year 1900 was the day of premiums—"save the coupons and get a premium." One of the popular songs of the time was "Today is the day they give babies away with a pound of te-*a*." The year 1900 was also the time that wagon retailing was at its height. Wagon retailers went from house to house selling tea, coffee, spices, milk, ice, meats, vegetables, medicines, and many other products. Later, with the coming of the motor truck some fairly complete grocery stores were operated in trucks. However, these "rolling" or truck stores did not usually prove successful. Their expenses were too high for their volume of sales.

CHAPTER II

1900–1917—High Cost of Living Era

Rise of Living Costs

The period from 1900 to 1917 may be characterized as the "high cost of living" era. Prices were going up faster than wages and so there was widespread outcry against the high cost of living although some editors by 1906 were asking if it was not "the cost of high living," showing that the standard of living was rising. During the latter part of this period (1915–1918) there was such an outcry against the high cost of living that commissions were appointed in several cities to find the reason and suggest remedies. It was common to blame the trouble on "too many middlemen," or upon the "high cost of marketing." The reports of some of these commissions are interesting in retrospect. One said that a part of the trouble came from buying packaged goods at higher prices and recommended to the consumers that they buy bulk goods which were cheaper. This report aroused the ire of national advertisers whose goods were usually sold in packages. Their fear of the report being followed appears to have been groundless. Other reports urged the establishment of more farmer markets where the farmer could sell direct to the consumers and eliminate all middlemen. For large cities, the use of curb markets was suggested; there retailers could sell foods without having to pay rent. Others recommended more consumer cooperative stores and buying clubs.

Looking back, all these recommendations seem rather foolish. The sale of packaged foods continued to increase until—aside from fruits, vegetables, and meats—very few unpackaged foods are now sold in retail stores. Farmers' retail markets have continued to decline in use, although a temporary slight increase was noted after the farmers bought motor trucks. In spite of all the propaganda and government aid, consumers' cooperatives now do less than 1 percent of the retail business of the country. I do not recall that any of these commissions recommended the growth of vertically integrated companies, self-serve stores, or one-story warehouses handling goods mechanically.

Improvements in the physical handling of goods—particularly by the railroads—were, however, in the minds of businessmen and government agencies. Traffic increased so fast during this period with industrial and farm expansion that many railroads were unable to move it expeditiously; and when the demands of a warring world were added, the railroads were so badly smothered with freight that the federal government undertook their operation.

Wholesaling

With the building of the railroad network in the 1870's and 1880's, the wholesalers spread out from the seaport and river towns into the interior. The thirty years from 1880 to 1910 may be said to have been the heyday of the wholesalers. The western country was filling up with people and new retail stores were being opened. The wholesalers thus had new stores to stock as well as established stores to supply. As a shrewd observer said, "Stocks in wholesale houses were profitable investments, usually yielding from 10 to 20 per cent dividends; however, after 1910 competition was so keen and profits so much lower that I sold all my wholesale stocks." After 1900 the rise of local wholesalers was rapid. To illustrate, there were in Illinois in 1900, twenty-five towns having wholesale grocers while in 1929 there were seventy-six such towns.[*] The small, country, county-seat trading-center town where I lived had three wholesalers in 1900 (two grocers and one drygoods). By 1907 this town had nine wholesalers, including three semijobbers (three grocers, three drygoods, two hardware, and one hat). Competition became so keen that the grocers solicited business from the town retailers daily.

[*] Fred M. Jones, *Grocery Wholesaling in Illinois from 1900 to 1929*, Bull. No. 36 (University of Illinois, Bureau of Business Research).

Retailing

The two typical retail stores were the general and the specialty stores in the small villages and towns, with the general stores disappearing as the size of the towns increased. The drygoods stores shaded into department stores. The latter were well established in the larger cities. Chain stores were growing especially in the latter part of the period.

During at least the first part of this period there seemed to be a fairly definite price structure which allowed a relatively well established margin and prices for the wholesalers. The retailers often bought from the salesmen they liked the best. The popular salesmen often "owned" a good deal of their trade and could take it with them if they changed to another wholesaler. The idea that retailers could originate their own orders and so dispense with the weekly or monthly calls of the salesmen was almost unknown and seemed an impossibility. It was not until competition with the chains became severe during the next period that retailers could be persuaded to write out and mail their orders. Butler Brothers, mail-order wholesaler of variety goods, supplied an exception to this statement.

Mail-Order Houses and Chain Stores

The mail-order houses were growing. I recall a Sears Roebuck catalog of about 1898 which carried a slogan across the top of the page: "Lowest prices on earth." The rural and small-town retailers were very bitter against the mail-order houses, not so much because of the loss of sales as the fact that many times daily their customers told them: "We can get it cheaper at Sears Roebuck." Parcel post service, started in 1913 (the law was passed on August 24, 1912), was a great help to the mail-order houses.

The chains were not important in 1900 except the variety chains and perhaps the grocery chains in a few eastern cities. The grocery chains, however, were beginning to grow. The first modern "cash carry" grocery store is said to have been established in 1908 and the Great Atlantic and Pacific Tea Company [A & P] which began business in 1859 started their "economy" stores in 1913. By the end of this period chains were important in food, drug, variety, shoe, and some other fields, and the retailers throughout the country were feeling their competition.

Railroading

Although the railroad network had been completed by 1893, a few trunk lines were built during this period—notably the Western Pacific from Salt Lake City to San Francisco; the San Pedro, Los Angeles, and Salt Lake (now Union Pacific); the Virginian, to haul coal from southern West Virginia to Hampton Roads; the Clinchfield (CC&O), connecting the eastern Kentucky coal fields to the Carolinas; the Louisville and Nashville, building from eastern Kentucky to Atlanta; and the Chicago, St. Paul, and Milwaukee, extending its track from South Dakota to Seattle. Most of the railroad development was in improving road beds, tracks, and terminals. The Pennsylvania and Grand Central terminals in New York, the union stations in Washington, St. Louis, and Kansas City were outstanding.

In 1900 freight trains usually consisted of fifteen or twenty cars and might have one, two, or three locomotives. Some of the "big, long trains" on the main trunk lines had as many as forty cars, but such trains had two or three locomotives. On the division of the Southern Railway where I lived it was common for a freight train to have two engines, some five or six cars, another engine, and then some ten or fifteen more cars and the caboose. Passenger trains had two to five cars. The through express "vestibule" had five wooden cars, and in the late 1890's was put on a forty-mile-an-hour schedule. Traffic increased. More cars were added. Heavier steel coaches came into use for their greater safety and the schedule was slowed down to thirty to thirty-five miles per hour for express trains, a schedule maintained for many years. Local passenger trains had schedules of around twenty-five miles per hour.

Locomotives were becoming larger. James J. Hill, of the Great Northern Railroad, was a pioneer in developing larger locomotives to get larger locomotives to haul longer trains. He said that he had advocated this because a man could not shovel coal through the firebox door for the longer firebox that would be required for bigger locomotives.

On the railroad where I lived, consolidation freight locomotives were introduced in 1906. They looked simply enormous. However, within six years they were relegated to switching and branch-line service and replaced by the much larger mikado locomotives for main-line freight service. Pacific-type passenger locomotives came into use for passenger service, replacing the ten-wheelers.

The answer for moving more freight was more tracks. The Pennsylvania had six tracks from Harrisburg to Philadelphia and four tracks from New York to Philadelphia and from Harrisburg to Pittsburgh. The New York Central had from four to six between New York and Buffalo. Electrification seemed a way of lessening the need for more tracks. The Milwaukee had electrified its track across the Rocky Mountains, the Norfolk & Western its steep Elkhorn grade west of Bluefield, and the suburban lines into Grand Central station and the tunnels under the Hudson River were electrified. The Pennsylvania had plans for electrifying its road over the Alleghenies between Altoona and Johnstown.

The mechanical stoker came into use during this period and made possible much larger locomotives and much longer trains. This meant that fewer trains could move the freight and there was less need for additional tracks. Rising wages made it more economical to buy larger locomotives than to pay two or three engine crews to move one train. The Norfolk & Western was said to have the largest supply of locomotives in relation to mileage and needs of any railroad in the country. However, by 1910 long rows of obsolete locomotives were standing idle and rusting in the Roanoke yards.

Growth of Central Power Stations

There had been notable improvements in boilers, turbines, and dynamos which meant that a kilowatt hour of electricity could be developed with less coal. Industries were finding it more economical to buy than to produce their own power. This has been particularly true since World War I. (In 1917, 3.4 lb coal to 1 KWH; in 1946, 1.3 lb coal to 1 KWH; and at this writing plants built in 1959 will use approximately 0.9 lb coal per 1 KWH.) Until World War I, the secular trend for coal production was up, after which it flattened out.

Prohibition

Maine and Kansas had been "dry" for several years and the prohibition laws appeared to work well. Prohibition spread rapidly in the Southeast in the early 1900's and into the Central and Far West by 1910. It was my observation and was generally claimed that prosperity increased in a town when it went dry. Much money formerly spent in saloons was spent in other stores, which increased their sales and stimulated the local economy. Also some of the town drunks sobered up and worked more steadily and more intelligently, thus increasing production. The incomes of the saloon keepers, brewers, and distillers suffered until they established new businesses. However, the stimulus to other businesses appeared to outweigh the injury done to the liquor trade. The same situation was observed in 1933 following "repeal." It was interesting that the opening of taverns, saloons, and bars gave business a "shot in the arm" which was more noticeable than the loss of sales by other types of business. Perhaps the explanation was that the newly established business offered employment to unemployed persons and increased their purchasing power while the established businesses did not immediately reduce the number of employees.*

Increase in Education

There had been a stronger interest in education following 1900 and the enrollment in both high schools and colleges increased. This included a growing interest in business education,

* It was said that the World's Fair stimulated business in the Chicago area in 1933 and 1934. It was pointed out that if people spent their vacations visiting the fair that other vacation places would suffer. Nevertheless the stimulus in one area was more noticeable than declines in sales in many widely scattered areas.

and it was in this period that many colleges of commerce and business administration were established.

The development of accounting techniques was notable. When the United States Steel Corporation was formed in 1901, many persons said that it could not succeed primarily because no man could carry all the information necessary for its operation in his head. The development of accounting, however, gave to the business executives factual information which enabled them to manage much larger enterprises than had been possible when they secured their information from first-hand observation. Improved accounting methods made the growth of large chain stores possible by enabling them to check on operations of their various stores. This "statistical control" was a major factor in business development in the period under consideration.

There was also a marked improvement in the quality of medical education. There were many so-called "sunset" medical colleges, in which practicing doctors lectured to the students who graduated with little or no hospital experience. In 1900 less than one-fourth of the medical schools required a high school education for entrance. Under the leadership of the Rockefeller Foundation, standards of medical education were raised and practical experience in hospitals required of seniors and interns. Many of the "sunset" colleges which did not have adequate facilities were closed, the number of medical schools decreased from 160 in 1905 to 96 in 1915, and the number of graduates decreased from 5,606 in 1905 to 3,530 in 1915. The number of medical schools and graduates continued to decline until the early 1920's. There has recently been a slight increase in the number of medical schools and a considerable increase in the number of students. There are now over 70 schools with over 6,000 graduates annually. With the automobile and present hospital and clinical facilities one doctor can adequately care for many more patients than in the "horse and buggy days."

Pure Food Law

There was much agitation against impure foods in the years following 1900, and the Pure Food law was passed in 1906. Many dairies were improving the cleanliness of milk. The commercial pasteurization of milk was begun in Boston about 1905. It was used by most of the milk distributors in the large cities by 1920 and was generally used in the smaller towns by 1935. Pasteurization was accompanied by more careful inspection of dairy farms and milk plants. The glass milk bottle came into general use about 1900. The paper milk bottle was introduced for the store sale of milk in several eastern cities in the early 1930's. Pure milk and pure water did more than anything else (prior to the discovery of the sulfas and the antibiotics) to reduce the death rate. Pure milk was especially important in reducing infant mortality.

Truth in Advertising

There was an outcry against untruthful advertising, and the "truth in advertising" campaign was started by advertising journals and advertising clubs were established in many cities. Laws against untruthful advertising were passed in many states.

The H. J. Heinz Company provided an illustration of how a company can capitalize on current public opinion. The public at this time was conscious of impure, adulterated, and dirty foods. The Heinz Company advertised that its products were pure, that they were clean, and that no benzoate of soda or other preservatives were used in their products. The public was invited to inspect the Heinz plants to see that they were clean and that all their products were prepared under sanitary conditions. Their products were aggressively advertised and merchandised. The company grew in size and became one of the larger and one of the most widely and favorably known companies in the food field.

Increased Consumption of Fruits and Vegetables

There were some outstanding changes in the American diet following 1900. Probably the most important was the growing and widespread consumption of fresh fruits and vegetables. Figures show very important increases in the per capita consumption of these products.* This increased consumption together with the increased population of the cities placed a severe strain on terminal marketing facilities. Anyone who can recall the congestion on South Water Street in Chicago, on Dock Street in Philadelphia, or in the Washington market district in New York has a vivid picture of this condition. Conditions were little better in other large cities. However, during the latter part of this period a start was made in expanding and improving terminal facilities for handling produce.

Panic of 1907

The "panic" of 1907 was not one of the major depressions but it was serious. Sales slumped. Collections were slow. After the break in October of 1907 and during 1908, some weeks people were paid in full and some weeks they were not. This was generally said to be a money panic "generated in Wall Street." In many cities money was so scarce that the bank clearing houses issued certificates to supplement the available supply of money. Some employers paid their workers part in currency and part in certificates. The country had neither a central banking system nor an elastic currency. A central bank was needed so that individual banks could cash in on their notes receivable by rediscounting them with the central bank when they needed more money. The central bank could then issue currency on the basis of such assets and retire the currency from circulation when the notes were paid. The amount of money in circulation would thus vary with needs. The situation resulting from the panic of 1907 hastened the establishment of the Federal Reserve System in 1914. Its sponsors said that it would make another "money panic" impossible. The depression of 1907 was the last one referred to as a "panic." Later ones have been called "depressions" or "recessions."

* Per capita consumption of fresh fruits increased from 169 lbs in 1899 to 192 lbs in 1923. Omitting apples, the consumption of which decreased, the increase was from 58 to 121 lbs. E. G. Montgomery and C. H. Kardell, U. S. Department of Commerce, *Domestic Commerce Series No. 38* (Washington, D.C.: Government Printing Office, 1930).

Prices of Farm Products

The prices of farm products rose in the years following 1900, and there was no noticeable break during 1907 and 1908. At the time it was often said that "the farmers are better off than the businessmen." Prices continued to rise, and for the farmers the years from 1910 to 1914 were among the most prosperous peacetime years in American history—certainly prior to 1946.

The period 1910-1914 was later adopted as the base period in price support programs for farm products. It is human nature to consider one's best performance as "normal."

New Industries

In the period from 1900 to World War I, the big new innovations among products were the automobile and the moving picture. To show the pictures, many theaters were built. Automobiles were coming into more general use; the Ford Motor Company was started in 1903 and the famous Model-T was introduced in 1908. Although many rural roads were quagmires in rainy weather, there was some improvement in the highways. The Glidden Tours focused attention on the need for intercity surfaced roads.

These tours were used to demonstrate the practicality of cross-country travel by automobile and to test the performance of cars. Scout cars spent considerable time exploring roads to find ones which were passable for automobiles, or the ones most likely to be passable, and laying out routes. On the tours each day's run was scheduled and each car checked out in the morning and checked in the evening if and when it got to the check point. Thus prizes could be awarded for performance. I recall the tour in the fall of 1909 was from New York to Atlanta. Roads were dry and dusty. Most of the cars were on scheduled time when they passed through Virginia. The lead car had little dust. The amount of dust increased with the passing of each car. It was so bad when twenty or thirty had passed that if my memory is correct one person died of suffocation before reaching Atlanta. The next spring on the run north rain and mud were encountered. Only one car, a light roadster that could be lifted back onto the road when it skidded off, was on time when the Shenandoah Valley was reached.

The social desirability of automobiles was widely discussed in this and in the following decade. It was said that many families who could not afford them bought cars; that people mortgaged their homes to buy cars; and that the automobile business hurt other businesses. Many retailers were skeptical if not openly hostile to cars, feeling that people spent money for automobiles that otherwise would have been spent with them. However, when the ownership of cars became widespread in the late 1920's, it was found that people had maintained their standard of eating and dressing and had as good houses and furniture as they had had before the advent of the automobile. That is, they had maintained their previous standard of living and added the automobile to it. This was made possible by the increased industrial production—that is, the increased output per worker. By the middle 1920's, the consumer summed up his decision on the automobile: "It costs a lot, but it's worth it." A statistical-minded friend of mine kept detailed records and came up with the figure of $22 and some cents a month as the total cost of having and operating a Ford car. I think he was about right. In the late 1920's, with less detailed records, I came up with the approximate figure of over $1 per day to cover repairs, license fee, insurance, gasoline, and oil on a six-cylinder car. This was "a lot of money" for the average man in the 1920's, "but it was worth it."

During the 1900's the telephone came into much more general use; both domestic and industrial use of electricity increased; the gasoline engine came into use; farm implements became larger and better; washing machines (both hand and power) increased in importance as did mechanical irons (charcoal, gasoline, and electric); vacuum cleaners began to be used; aluminum cooking utensils were introduced; cold storage warehouses increased in number; municipal water plants and sewage disposal plants spread to the smaller cities; and central heating plants became common in better homes. In the latter part of the period motor trucks and tractors began to be used. Wireless came into use to communicate with ships at sea, and the airplane was in the experimental stage. Rayon was in the introductory stage.

Trust Movement

A matter of great public interest in the 1900's was the "Trust Movement." The cartoonists liked to portray President Theodore Roosevelt with his "big stick," a club like that of "Jack the Giant Killer," lambasting the trusts which were portrayed as big fat businessmen. There were many consolidations and mergers of business concerns around the beginning of the century—the United States Steel Corporation, the Standard Oil Company, the American Tobacco Company, and the International Harvester Company, to mention only a few. The industrial development consisted of the appearance of large numbers of small factories, many of which were merged into larger corporations during the 1880's and 1890's. There were various reasons for such consolidations—the founders wanted to sell out and take their profits and retire; small companies were often too small to afford the sales organization and advertising necessary to attain a profitable sales volume; many of the early small factories were less efficient than their larger competitors. In some instances goods can be produced at lower unit costs in large plants—the overworked "law of decreasing costs." More often a company becomes large because it is efficient rather than becoming efficient because it is large. In any event there were many consolidations.

Competition sometimes led to the cutting of prices to unprofitable levels. This was especially true among the railroads with their high fixed expenses. To avoid competition leading to unprofitable prices, price agreements were often made between competitors. These were often called "gentlemen's agreements." However, some of the parties to such agreements were not "gentlemen," and in most cases these agreements were soon broken. A device was developed by which the stock of competing companies was placed in trust and the businesses managed in whole or part by the trustees. This practice became so common that the word "trust" came into general use to denote monopolies or attempts to secure monopoly power. There were so many such combines that the Sherman antitrust law was passed in 1890.

The rash of mergers in the early 1900's led to considerable activity by the Department of Justice in bringing antitrust suits. These led to the dissolution of the Northern Securities Company, the Standard Oil Company, and the American Tobacco Company. President Roosevelt established the Bureau of Corporations to study and report on corporate growth and restraints of competition. Under President Woodrow Wilson, this formed the nucleus of the Federal Trade Commission which was to help prevent restraints of trade and unfair competition. Much was heard at this time of the "twilight zone," the hazy borderline between that which was legal and that which was illegal.

President Wilson expressed the hope that the Trade Commission would help businessmen to determine in advance what practices were legal and what ones were illegal and so prevent law violations. This hope was not realized. Too often a businessman when told that a practice *may* be legal, or that it is of doubtful legality, will go ahead and adopt the practice and say that "the Government told me to do this." The Clayton act was also passed to strengthen the Sherman law; it was to be enforced in part by the Department of Justice and in part by the Federal Trade Commission. The Trade Commission has been of great importance in lessening restraints on competition and in preventing bad practices, particularly those involving untruthful advertising and misrepresentation of goods sold in interstate commerce. The Commission's two main activities included: (1) investigating the operations and practices of business and publishing the facts for the use of Congress, state legislatures, economists, and the public; and (2) conducting hearings and issuing "cease and desist" orders against business concerns found to be using unfair and illegal practices, and then appealing to the courts for enforcement when their orders were not obeyed.

Passing of the Barons

The closing decades of the nineteenth and the first decade of the twentieth century saw the business barons in their glory—John D.

Rockefeller, J. P. Morgan, Andrew Carnegie, H. C. Frick, Commodore Vanderbilt, Jay Gould, James J. Hill, E. H. Harriman, Andrew Mellon, and dozens of others with equal and lesser domains. When the century opened, Rockefeller was completing his oil empire. Carnegie was hunting a buyer for his steel mills. Commodore Vanderbilt and Jay Gould had built their railway systems; J. P. Morgan, the financial wizard, was at the height of his power; and Andrew Mellon was welding together the Mellon mining, oil, manufacturing, and banking empire. Harriman was putting together his Union—Southern Pacific railroad systems and in 1901 engaged in his famous fight with Hill for control of the Northern Pacific and Burlington railways.*

This was the period of "tainted money" when churches turned down gifts from Rockefeller on the basis that the money was made dishonestly and hence was tainted. A story of this time is that of the church which was raising money in the good old Methodist way of soliciting subscriptions in public meeting. First the names of those who would give $100, then those who would give $50, and on down to $25, $10, and $5. As the subscriptions lagged short of the goal a man in the back arose and said: "Here is a dollar I won in a poker game. Will you take it?" The preacher snapped: "Give it to the Lord. The devil has had it long enough."

The World War I period marked the end of the dominance of business by the barons. This was in part due to the enforcement of the Sherman and Interstate Commerce laws, the passing of the Clayton act, but perhaps in greater part by an aroused public opinion against "malefactors of great wealth." Most of the barons were personally honest. They took care of their men and they expected their men to be loyal to them. Somewhat the flavor of the old feudal system, of "noblesse oblige," was to be found. An older worker of the U. S. Steel Corporation during the labor trouble in the early 1920's said: "I fought for the Company at Homestead in 1892 and if need be I will fight for it again." All men, particularly the executives, were expected to be loyal to their employers and in turn the employers were expected to take care of them. The barons did not, however, have any great feeling of *general social* obliga-

* The fight ended in a draw.

tion. Business units had been small, and in such units there was usually no great consciousness of social obligation. Classical economic theory taught that if each person did that which was best for himself the result would be best for society. When companies became large, it took a generation for them to realize that they had a general social obligation in addition to their specific obligation to the owners and the employees.

The top executive of 1910 was usually a self-made man managing a company he had built or in which he owned a substantial interest. He was a man of relatively little formal education who had started as an office boy, clerk, or factory worker and who had fought his way up against stiff competition. He based his decisions largely on his own experiences, observations, and the advice of his subordinates. He was proud of his success and jealous of his position. He lived in a mansion and had a number of servants. He had no income tax to pay.

My opinion is that a very large part of the criticism of the barons came from their display of wealth. The term "conspicuous consumption"* was coined to cover such display—large mansions, glamorous parties, social position based on wealth as reflected in the term "the four hundred." I recall the papers carrying the story that the flowers for one such party cost $25 thousand. This was more money than the average professional man, retailer, or farmer accumulated in a lifetime. This was, to say the least, bad taste in a democracy. These men were "noveau rich" and they wanted the world to know of their success.

The barons, nevertheless, contributed much to the development of the country and its welfare. Cyrus McCormick developed the reaper and later the binder and made farming much easier and more profitable. John D. Rockefeller brought oil to the people in even the remotest regions, and the oil lamp was a great improvement over the candle. Andrew Carnegie made steel cheaper than it has ever been made in the history of the world—either before or since. Commodore Vanderbilt welded together an excellent railroad system, but was probably more widely known for saying "the public be damned." Harriman was said to have made a $100 mil-

* This term is generally attributed to Thorstein Veblen.

lion out of his railroads, but when he bought a railroad he improved it physically to keep up with the demands of a growing country and to give good service to shippers and travelers. Jim Hill, who built a great railroad without government subsidy, was known as an "empire builder" for his development of a big slice of the northwestern territory. In addition to these industrial advancements, much of the money of the barons eventually went to colleges, universities, libraries, medical and educational foundations, churches, art galleries, parks, and theological seminaries.

One of the great changes in business during the past forty years has been the change in the type of business executive. The top executive of the 1950's is usually a college graduate, with perhaps a Beta Gamma Sigma key or other emblem of scholastic attainment. He has had courses in applied economics or business and very likely also in social economics. He takes government regulations more or less as a matter of course. His problem is to live with the regulations whether or not he approves of them, and the same is true of labor unions. He depends a great deal on information obtained from his accountants, research men, and statisticians. He may have a staff of experts to recommend policies based on the findings of researchers. Often he does not own the company he manages and may own very little stock in it. He is a professional manager, but he has a much greater sense of social responsibility than did the executive of 1900.

On the other side, he does not have the zest for a competitive struggle as did his predecessor. He believes more in administered and stabilized prices. He often overlooks the fact that his unit cost might be much lower if his sales were higher.

In the 1900's it was often said that a "man could not make a million dollars honestly." Then along came Henry Ford and proved the fallacy of this statement. He made the best product of his time, sold it at the lowest price, paid the highest wages, and made the most money. The example of Henry Ford was heralded from platform and pulpit where it formerly had been the fashion to berate "the malefactors of great wealth." In contrast to many of the business barons, Henry Ford was an industrious, family man who cared relatively little for "conspicuous consumption."

Henry Ford and the Assembly Line

Henry Ford started in 1903 to make an automobile which the man of average means could afford. He made profits from the first. In 1908 he came out with the famous Model-T—one product, one color, and at what seemed to be ever lower prices (down to $295) to reach an ever larger market. This was the outstanding example of simplification (commonly called "standardization" at the time) and mass production. Henry Ford pioneered new methods of factory production, arrangement, and work organization. He won much fame for the $5-a-day minimum wage, more than most skilled workers, salesmen, and many professional and businessmen were making at the time. But to earn the high wage a high standard of performance was required.

In 1915 whenever factory executives pointed out the latest or best method of operation, they almost always pointed to the Ford factory at Highland Park. The most notable and most widely copied was the assembly line aspect. This has come to be generally used in factories, wholesale houses, etc., and may almost be said to be the method used in present-day supermarkets. The assembly-line idea has been copied around the world, and Henry Ford probably has influenced the world more than any other American of the past seventy-five years, with the possible exception of Woodrow Wilson.

Ford was reported to have made a billion dollars from the Model-T from 1908 to 1917. The Ford Motor Company came to have the best dealer and service garage organization in the country, thanks largely to James Couzens, the sales manager, later a U. S. Senator. Henry Ford could probably have been elected President in 1920 if he had campaigned a little and called upon his dealers for active support. They were willing, and Ford wanted to be President, but he stood aloof wanting to be drafted.

Ford stuck to the Model-T too long. When highways were paved, the consumers wanted faster cars. General Motors and other car manufacturers passed Ford in quality. When Ford decided to change to a gearshift car, he attempted the change too suddenly. Errors were made and the Ford car was off the market for almost two years. His dealer organization deteriorated. From a colossal success to a colossal fiasco! Ford never recovered his reputation for business acumen or his great popularity with the people.

Theory of High Wages

Wages were rising. A new theory—that high wages were good for business because they gave the working man increased purchasing power and so increased sales—was advocated by a radical businessman here and there, and the theory was discussed in university classrooms. This theory was used in the 1920's by the labor unions in arguing for higher wages and was adopted by the "New Deal" administration in the 1930's in "putting over" the National Recovery Administration (NRA).

It is increased production, however, that increases purchasing power. Higher wages without increased output would not increase total purchasing power. If the pay of all workers is raised and the increase in cost is passed on as higher prices, then the workers will benefit only to the extent that nonworkers (*e.g.*, pensioners, property owners) are injured. Total purchasing power is not immediately increased because society can buy only the same quantity of goods and services. However, the sale of goods might increase as the workers may spend more and save less than some other groups. This might be bad in the long run as the supply of capital for industrial growth would be curtailed. Again, rising wages may cause employers to develop and introduce labor-saving devices and so increase the output per worker. Here the argument becomes involved. Is the important incentive the higher wages or the desire for larger profits?

The demand for higher pay is a natural one. The group pushing for higher wages wants its purchasing power increased. It is not particularly interested in other groups getting higher wages. The *trade* union may strive for higher wages for its members but may be opposed to higher wages for other groups of workers since such increase in wages is likely to result in higher prices which would have to be paid by members of the trade union.

CHAPTER III

1917–1921—World War I and the Ensuing Depression

Wartime Controls

America, up to the World War I period, had been dependent upon Europe for several manufactured products, particularly chemicals. The war in Europe cut America off almost entirely from synthetic dyes and the country had to develop a dye industry of its own. The United States record of production for World War I was not good in many lines. Many of the American troops in Europe depended upon European guns. The building of ships at Hog Island and in other yards was very disappointing. However, the stimulus to manufacturing resulting from war demands led to a great development of American factories and to great "know-how" of production methods which made possible the so-called "new industrial revolution of the 1920's."

Following the outbreak of war in Europe in the summer of 1914, the United States suffered a slight recession. By the spring of 1915 it was evident that the war would last a considerable time, and the warring countries placed large orders for munitions in the United States. Winning the war was the object, and prices were secondary. Plants had to be built and manufacturers protected against a sudden stopping of orders. France and England bid against each other. The index of wholesale prices started to rise in October 1915 and rose 67 percent by April 1917 when the United States entered the war. There was a great outcry against the high prices. Consumer "strikes" against this or that commodity occurred and there was talk of bread riots. High wages were paid in some munitions plants but wages and salaries in general lagged far behind prices. There was need for price control. The United States had absolutely no machinery for this and little knowledge of how to control prices.

Nevertheless, laws were passed and organizations established. These met with considerable success as prices rose only 19 percent from April 1917 to November 1918 when the war ended.

There was also an outcry against profiteers and there were patriotic appeals to be satisfied with fair profits. Prices were fixed by the government on many commodities. The prevailing theory of price determination was the marginal theory. An application of this, the "bulk-line theory," was generally used by government boards in fixing prices, although the cost-plus theory was used on many government purchases and contracts. Typical procedure under the bulk-line method was to gather costs from the producers and then set the price high enough to allow the "bulk" or major portion of the product to be sold without a loss. The proportion of the output allowed a profit depended upon the need for the goods. For copper, which was a badly needed munition, the price was set over 100 percent to bring submarginal (high cost) mines into production, while for lumber the figure might be 60 percent as the desire was to curtail all construction not directly connected with the war effort.

Break in Prices

The almost universal opinion among businessmen was that prices were too high and that they would come down with the end of the war. The armistice was signed on November 11, 1918. The wholesale price index dropped 5 percent between November and February. There was, however, a pent up demand for houses, furniture, household appliances, and automobiles; and prices started up in February and rose 29 percent in sixteen months in the period to May 1920. In dollars and cents the prices of an average list of commodities rose four-fifths as much in these sixteen months as in the nineteen months from October 1915 to April 1917. The first significant indication of a break came in the price of silk on the Japanese silk bourse in the early spring of 1920. Prices reached their peak in May 1920, but the "break" came in July. Prices broke sharply, the wholesale index declining 26 percent from July to December and 43 percent from May 1920 to May 1921, when the price level was back to where it had been in November 1916.

This was the much publicized "buyers' strike." The idea was that people still had purchasing power but that they refused to buy at the existing high prices. The edge had been taken off the demand for new houses. Some merchants had large stocks and were afraid to carry them over the summer and offered large discounts at their winter clearance sales. (I recall buying a nationally advertised overcoat that had been priced at $65.00 for $27.50 in February.) Prices of several farm products tumbled in July with slackening European demand. Once prices started their decline, the consumers waited for further declines. This was logical in view of widespread belief that prices were too high. Thus 1920, which started as a boom year, ended in a serious depression.

The break in prices was much more rapid in some commodities than in others. For example, the refiner's price of sugar dropped from 21¢–22½¢ on August 11, to 11¢ on October 10. This resulted in a heavy loss to many grocers, and many wholesalers might have been ruined except for large surpluses earned during the war years. One retailer ordered a carload of sugar, and by the time it was delivered it had fallen $5 thousand in value. This was more than his net worth and would have ruined him except for the fact that the sugar had been damaged in transit so that he could reject it.

A man had decided to start manufacturing paper boxes and had ordered his machines and two carloads of cardboard. By the time they arrived the price had dropped so much that he was insolvent. Nevertheless, he started the business and became very successful.

A shoe factory had been very profitable, but as one executive said, "We became insolvent one night in November owing to the drop in the price of leather and other products. One item purchased by the carload dropped from 42¢ to 16¢. If we had gone into bankruptcy we would have carried at least one tanner with us. I conferred with the bank and they agreed to carry us if I would stay with the company until the debt was paid. This required seven years." This was the period (1920–1921) of "frozen assets." Frozen assets were made up of stocks of goods which could not be sold immediately or of accounts which could not be collected until the merchants collected from their customers.

The depression of 1921 was very serious. I lived in Pittsburgh at the time. Many of the steel mills were closed, their stacks rusting, and unemployment was high. Although this was a severe depression, it was also a very short one. Prices came down enough to end the "buyers' strike" while the consumers still had some reserve purchasing power. More houses were needed and people were buying automobiles in quantity.

Price Guarantees

To restore confidence, many manufacturers and dealers adopted the policy of guaranteeing their prices. This was extended not only to the dealers but also to the consumers. The Ford Motor Company, which was a leader in this policy, deserves a great deal of credit for its part in getting people to buying and so improving business. People wanted cars and other things but hesitated to buy because prices might drop further. By guaranteeing the prices, sellers got the consumers to buying in quantity. I recall buying a piece of furniture in the spring of 1921 and in the late summer receiving a check for $5 because the price had dropped.

The Federal Trade Commission, however, was critical of the policy of guaranteeing prices, charging that having made such guarantees the manufacturers would be very loath to further reduce prices. Charges and investigations were made. However, rapidly improving business conditions in 1922 seem to have put an end to these.

Recovery

The recovery in 1922 was very rapid. A salesman for a company selling building materials during the last week in April said that every salesman in the Pittsburgh territory had already passed his 1922 sales quota. It is not much of an exaggeration to say that manufacturers were calling men back to work in the mills while they were still laying off men from their office and engineering staffs. The year 1922 was a prosperous one.

The year 1921 was a year of "hand-to-mouth" or small-order buying. Merchants had suffered heavy losses on inventories, and when this is the case they then buy in smaller quantities. One would suppose that hand-to-mouth buying would cause higher rates of stock turnover in the following years. This, however, did not generally occur. Apparently the retailers used the freed capital to carry more diversified stocks, especially a wider assortment of colors. Having developed a dye industry of their own, American manufacturers went on a "color spree." Clothing became more colorful. Many kinds of goods—from automobiles to stoves and plumbing fixtures—appeared in a variety of colors.

CHAPTER IV

1922–1929—New Industrial Revolution

Increase in Output per Worker

The period from 1922 to 1929 was often called the "New Industrial Revolution."* Manufacturers had acquired more plants, "know-how," confidence, and new machines during the first World War. The morale of the workers, on the whole, was high, and output per worker increased.

The government turned the railroads back to their owners in 1920. The general feeling was that the railroads would be given one more chance to operate their lines and supply adequate transportation to the country, and then, if they did not do so, the government would take them over permanently. The railroads were thus under the necessity of improving their service. This they did. First they had to restore their roadways and equipment and then improve and speed up their service. They succeeded so well that by the end of the decade very little more was heard of the possibility of government ownership and operation. During this decade there was some development of the diesel locomotive, particularly by the Burlington railroad.

Air transportation of mail was established about 1921 and that of passengers begun.

The central station production of electricity grew rapidly. The increased efficiency of the boilers and generating equipment was

* Estimates of output per worker vary with the method used in making the computations and often show sharp changes from one year to another. One estimate shows an increase in output per man-hour in manufacturing of 31 percent from 1922 to 1929; contrasted with this was 20 percent from 1914 to 1921 and 14 percent from 1930 to 1937. The percentages will, however, vary with the years selected for comparison. National Bureau of Economic Research figures quoted in National Association of Manufacturers, *Series No. 53* (September 1952).

phenomenal. The coal mining industry suffered, on the other hand. Industries in an ever-increasing number found that they could buy power cheaper than they could produce it.

The 1920's saw many new products come into general use. Several of these had been pioneered in the preceding decade. Foremost was the building of highways and the increased number of automobiles and motor trucks. Tractors came into use, and farm tractors needed different implements—larger implements and ones that could be operated from the tractor seat. Much of the old farm machinery was replaced. Radios were an entirely new product that came into general use during this decade. Mechanical home refrigerators were introduced and were sold in large numbers. There was an increase in the use of other household appliances such as washing machines, water heaters, domestic furnaces, vacuum cleaners, electric irons, fans.

Consumers came to spend a much larger proportion of their incomes on durable goods. "Consumer durables" became an important factor in the economy. The difference between good times and bad times is pretty much the difference in expenditures for durable goods by industry and the household consumers. Consumption of perishable goods like food, clothing, tobacco, and household fuel is pretty much the same in good times and bad. Prior to the 1920's the principal durables, aside from houses and furniture, were industrial goods such as factories, railroads, mines, and various kinds of machines and equipment. Durable goods do not have to be replaced at any particular time. Their purchase is irregular. More are purchased in good times than in bad times. The increased importance of consumer durables added another unsettling factor to the economy—a factor that can make booms go higher and allow depressions to go lower. To meet this situation more marketing research was and is needed, and business executives need to be market minded.

The dye and chemical industries grew rapidly. The production and use of rayon increased greatly.

Filling stations, service garages, and radio shops became common. Tourist cabins and motels were being established to accommodate the ever-increasing number of motorists.

Research

An interesting development during the 1920's was the increasing interest in research—technical research and marketing research. Although technical research does not come within the scope of this discussion, it was tremendously important. The main interest in marketing research was in market analysis or in determining potential markets and setting sales quotas. In fact, in the early 1920's it was usually called "market analysis."

During the 1920's interest developed in consumer surveys, and questionnaire and sampling techniques were developed largely by the people making marketing surveys. The switch in emphasis from market potentials to consumer surveys was due no doubt to the necessity of the seller's knowing what products and services the consumers wanted. It no longer sufficed to know how many consumers there were, where they lived, and how much money they had.*

Another sign of the growing interest in marketing research was the demand for a census of distribution. Sample censuses were taken in a number of cities in 1927 covering 1926, and in 1930 for the first time a national census of distribution was taken covering the year 1929, both under the leadership of Herbert Hoover. This was a real landmark in the development of factual information in the field of marketing.

Two notable studies included an analysis of chain stores by the Federal Trade Commission from 1929 to 1934, and the Louisville Grocery Survey conducted by the United States Department of Commerce in the late 1920's.

Several university bureaus of business research had become active, and by 1922 a very considerable amount of information was available on the expenses and profits of several kinds of retail and wholesale stores.

* This change was well illustrated in two books by Percival White. His 1921 book, *Market Analysis*, dealt primarily with methods of computing market potentials, while his 1931 book, *Marketing Research Technique*, dealt largely with consumer surveys made by personal interviews. It contained only a brief and elementary treatment of sampling; the art, or science, of sampling had not yet developed.

The interest in marketing research continued to develop in the 1930's. Many companies became interested in research when their sales dropped or when they were operating at a loss. Interest developed in buying motives, consumer desires, product design, trading areas, analysis of distribution costs, store location, consumer opinions (political polls, as an example), brand preferences, readership of advertisements, influence of advertisements, sales potentials, quota setting, demand for new products, and other subjects.

An outstanding success of the 1930's was the development of indexes of retail sales of food and drug items by the A. C. Nielsen Company. These indexes supply information on the retail sales of selected articles by brand names. From this information manufacturers can know the retail sales of their goods and can compare them with sales of competitors in various territories and in various types of stores. This enables them to know if they are gaining or losing their share of the market. Later, diaries—or purchase records kept by panels of consumers selected to give a cross-section of the population—were useful in securing information on retail purchases and other aspects of the markets.

Prohibition

Prohibition, moonshining, and bootlegging should be mentioned. The prohibition forces probably unwisely decided to force prohibition on the entire country. The large industrial and metropolitan areas were not ready for it. Many of the workers in these areas were recent immigrants from eastern and southern Europe who had been largely untouched by the moral propaganda against the use of alcohol. The demand in these metropolitan areas was so strong that the federal government was unable to prevent widespread bootlegging. Enforcement had broken in these areas to such an extent that by the close of the decade many people were seriously asking if the benefits of prohibition outweighed the evils of bootlegging and its accompanist—the gangster. The amendment was repealed in 1933. Saloons, taverns, distilleries, and breweries quickly opened giving an immediate increase in employment. Money spent on liquor hurt other businesses which had to reduce employment. The reduction in employment in injured businesses was much slower, however, than the increase in employment in the liquor industries, with the result that the economy was given a temporary "shot-in-the-arm" by repeal.

Motor Age

Another basic change which affected the marketing structure fundamentally was the coming into general use of automobiles. The ownership of cars had been more widespread during the decade 1910–1920. Progress was being made on improving roads and highways so that automobiles could be used the year round. The closed car came into use, and my recollection is that in 1923 the sale of closed cars ("limousine and sedan" types) passed the sale of open or touring car types.

The finance companies had a rapid growth in the early 1920's. The credit man for a large bank said: "Those fellows are up and down the street and in every bank every day borrowing every cent they can." The banks were willing to loan on buyers' notes endorsed by the dealers or finance companies but were unwilling to make direct loans to the people buying cars. Their conservatism apparently caused them to "miss a good boat."

The period of the 1920's was the great era of highway building and of bringing automobiles into almost universal use, at least in the rural areas and smaller towns of the country. In fact, many people attributed most of the prosperity to the building of automobiles and highways and said that the depression starting with the stock market crash in October 1929 was caused by the end of a highway building era—just as the depression of 1893 had marked the end of the building of the railways, and that of 1837 had marked the end of building canals.

Truck transportation also became important. A notable contribution was the general introduction of pneumatic truck tires in the middle 1920's. During the war the railroads were unable to move freight expeditiously. During the war winter of 1917–1918 some freight was moved from Detroit to New York by truck. This was a very severe winter, and highways were covered with ice and snow. This attempt was such a failure that it was generally believed that the intercity movement of freight by truck was absolutely impractical. However, by 1922 there existed a considerable amount of intercity motor truck movement of freight, and in the 1930's the motor truck became a major freight carrier.

The automobile changed life fundamentally, more than anything since the building of the railroads. The automobiles spread cities out, led to an increased development of suburbs, increased the number of branch stores, and led many workers to build their homes along the highways in the open country.*

The automobile changed retailing. At first it tended to centralize trade. There was less need for neighborhood stores, and the food chains discontinued many of their neighborhood stores. Rural people often bypassed the rural and village stores and went to the county seat towns to trade. In the early 1920's the prediction was frequently made that the small agricultural villages would soon disappear. It was to check the accuracy of this statement that I became interested in rural retailing and the movement of retail trade. My first study was made in 1926–1927 and showed that the sales of village stores in Illinois were declining but at a much slower rate than generally supposed. Two later studies have been made of rural retailing in Illinois, the last extending up to 1950.†

---

* Of course there had previously been much of this. In the early days of the republic, many of the lawyers and doctors had their offices on their farms and some courthouses had only a few houses about them. By the end of the nineteenth century, however, most professional men seemed to have located in the towns. Some workers still lived in the country. I recall in my home community that some of the carpenters, masons, harnessmakers, watch repairmen, blacksmiths, and stonecutters lived from one to four miles in the country and walked back and forth to work.

In the 1920's large numbers of factory workers lived in the country. My attention was called to the Anderson-Muncie-Newcastle community in Indiana and to the Lansing area in Michigan. However, these were not particularly unusual.

† P. D. Converse, *The Automobile and the Village Merchant* (1927); Robert V. Mitchell, *Trends in Rural Retailing in Illinois, 1928–1938;* and Donald W. Scotton, *Trends in Rural Retailing in Two Illinois Districts, 1938 to 1950;* all published by the Bureau of Business Research [or by the Bureau of Economic and Business Research] of the University of Illinois. A fourth

The business of the small villages, under 800 population, has declined greatly unless the village is on a main highway and gets enough business from filling stations, restaurants, motels, and garages to make up in loss from other lines. Medium-sized villages (population from 800 to 2500) have declined less while most towns of over 2500 population appear to have had at least a slight increase in business. However, relatively few villages have disappeared. Many of them have simply become residential suburbs for workers living in nearby larger towns.

When motorists first took to the road, they stopped at established hotels. As the number of motorists grew, many private families rented rooms to overnight guests and became "tourist homes." This practice started in the 1920's but became common in the early 1930's when many families needed additional income and many tourists had limited funds.

Many motorists carried camping equipment, and in the early 1920's towns vied with one another in establishing camps for motorists. In 1923 there were so many motorists in Yellowstone Park that a cartoonist pictured the bears holding a meeting to protest against the unfair competition of the campers in attracting too much attention and hurting the pride of the bears who considered themselves a main park attraction. With many unpaved roads, numerous detours, making and breaking camp, daily distances probably averaged less than 225 miles. Camping involved work, beds and meals were often poor, and there were discomforts especially in bad weather. The fad of camping passed almost as quickly as it came. It was followed later by the "trailer craze."

Tourist cabins started in the West, and by the middle 1930's they were common over the western half of the country and not unknown elsewhere. Motels (cabins with hotel-quality rooms and furnishings) started in California and were getting a foothold among the main western highways by the middle 1930's.

---

study, by P. D. Converse and Ramona Russell, "Why City Workers Live in Agricultural Villages," appeared in *Current Economic Comment,* published by this Bureau in August 1950.

Growing Up of the Chain Store

One of the most outstanding developments of the period was the growth of the chain stores. The decade of the 1920's may, from the marketing standpoint, be characterized as the chain store decade. During the rising price period, especially from 1915–1920, people had ever increasingly patronized the chain stores. Hundreds of new chains were started. Many of these were local chains and some of them were consolidated into larger organizations. The cash-carry method was becoming popular and was the method used by most of the chains. Successful retailers saw the establishment of additional stores as a practical way of expanding their businesses. One of the main problems of such retailers was securing the wholesale buying status and so becoming vertically integrated. As one grocer who made the transition said, "It was a question of breaking down the manufacturers one at a time until we had sufficient volume. Our first direct purchase was a carload of soap as the soap manufacturers had never adhered strictly to the wholesaler."

Without automobiles, if the consumers had to carry their groceries home, it was desirable that the stores be located close to them. With the use of automobiles, a neighborhood cash-carry store was no longer necessary. The Great Atlantic and Pacific Tea Company, having adopted the cash-carry plan wholeheartedly, was opening new stores as fast as new managers could be trained. They, at one time, had 16,000 stores and had announced that they expected to operate 20,000. However, with the automobile so many small stores were not needed. The cost of supervising small stores also became burdensome, particularly because of the higher wage rate prevailing in the 1920's. Near the end of the decade there was a definite trend toward larger stores.

The chains grew rapidly in the sale of women's dresses, coats, hats, and other soft goods. Chains of department stores grew, especially those handling popular-priced lines of goods. The chains could keep their buyers continually in New York and so could follow changes in fashions better than the individually operated stores which had to depend upon periodic visits of their buyers, and the assistance of resident buyers in New York.

Many of these chains adopted "central merchandising" under which plan unit stock records are kept in a central office; with daily reports of sales from each store, new styles ("hot numbers") can be gotten to the stores quickly and slow-selling numbers ("pups") discontinued promptly. Not all chains selling fashion goods use this system, although it was quite the vogue in the 1920's. Some groups of independent stores have adopted this system for popular-priced garments. The plan is operated by a resident buying office, either independent or store owned.

The growth of grocery chains attracted the most attention and the most opposition. Several of the early chains started by selling tea and coffee and gradually added other products in the 1890's and 1900's. The Great Atlantic and Pacific Tea Company, for example, added sugar in 1884 and baking powder in 1894.* A figure that sticks in my mind of the number of items handled by a typical chain grocery store in the 1910's was 484. In the 1920's, as the chains came to compete with each other and having saturated the market for the limited number of staples, they increased their stocks. By the close of the decade some chain stores carried larger assortments of goods than the competing independent stores.†

At this time, the most frequently mentioned advantages of the chains were: lower prices, cleaner stores, better-lighted stores, fresher goods, and more rapid stock turnover which accounted for fresher goods and helped to reduce the prices. Many consumers thought the independents could meet chain-store competition if they would clean up their stores, select their stocks better, turn their stocks faster, advertise better, and contrast personal salesmanship and friendship with the chain stores' impersonal treatment of customers. The wholesalers and retailers who competed with the chains realized that the chains could lay the goods down in their retail stores at lower cost than that of the traditional service wholesaler. This resulted from vertical integration and better

* Roy J. Bullock, *Harvard Business Review*, October 1933.

† One trade authority gives the following as typical of the number of items handled by food stores: 1928—867; 1950—3,750; 1957—5,144.

buying prices obtained by the chain from larger purchases and greater bargaining ability. To secure the same advantages of vertical integration, voluntary and retailer-owned wholesale houses came into the picture. The Federal Trade Commission's investigation of the chain stores began in 1929. Buying advantages were found in larger advertising and other allowances and discounts amounting to some 2 percent or 2½ percent of purchases. An object of passing the Robinson-Patman amendment to the Clayton act in 1936 was to make any such allowances available to all buyers on an equitable basis.

The most frequent criticisms made against the chain stores were: short-weighing and short-changing customers; underpaying employees; taking money out of the community; and failure to support the communities where they operated. It was found later that the chains paid employees somewhat better than the independents; but the figures were not strictly comparable as the manager of a chain store is an employee while the manager of an independent store is usually the owner and not an employee, so that his earnings are not included with store employees. With a few exceptions, the chains had very poor public relations programs, and by and large they had not supported the local communities. The chains operating small stores, such as shoe stores and dress shops, were usually the worst offenders. The chain-store owners claimed that the best service to the consumers was low prices. The wave of antichain legislation forced them to realize that low prices were not enough. They came to realize that everyone owes a duty to the community in which he lives or does business. The chains started active public relations programs and in the 1930's they greatly improved their public relations. The organizations operating chains of department and variety stores were leaders in this movement.

The antichain store propaganda was widespread and heated. Its strength can be indicated by the story of the schoolteacher in a small town who was discharged because she was seen to enter a chain store. The independent retailers clamored for legislation to protect them against the chains. Since there were a great many more of the retailers, they were more successful than had been the wholesalers who clamored against the auctions in the period following the War of 1812, or the city retailers who clamored against the department stores in the 1890's, or the rural retailers who had clamored against the mail-order houses in the 1900's. The independent retailers were successful in having laws passed in many states imposing higher taxes on the chain stores and in a smaller number of states passing laws against "loss-leader selling."

Competition by the Independent Retailers

On the whole, the laws against the chains were not effective in curtailing their growth. The independent retailers came to realize that if they were to meet chain-store competition they must do so by becoming more efficient and by reducing the cost of operating their stores. It was realized that if the independent retailer went out of business so would the independent wholesaler. One of the chief advantages of the chains was direct buying from the manufacturers and the operation of their own warehouses. They largely eliminated the expense of buying and selling functions between the wholesaler and retailer. Another advantage of the chain was the one advertisement which would cover all the stores located in a city. The wholesalers worked out a plan of securing these two advantages. They would have retailers originate their orders so that the wholesaler's salesmen would no longer be needed, and they would run advertisments in the city papers for all of the co-operating retailers. These organizations came to be known as voluntary chains. S. M. Flickinger of Buffalo was one of the pioneers in developing this form of organization—the Red and White stores. Many of the voluntary wholesalers in the 1920's were very loosely organized. The main advantage of many of them was that they enabled the independent retailers, usually grocers, to advertise in city papers at a reasonable cost. However, many voluntary chains disintegrated in the 1930's.

Retailer-owned wholesalers had started much earlier—the Frankford Company in Philadelphia as early as 1888, and the American Hardware and Supply Company in Pittsburgh in 1910. These organizations have grown more slowly since there was no strong incentive to get out and actively solicit new members. However, there are now a number of efficiently operated and successful retailer-owned wholesale houses in the food and hardware trades.

The chain stores have supervisors who check on the store managers to see that they carry out their instructions. They also give the store managers much information, advice, and help in operating their stores. Voluntary wholesalers tried to duplicate this service and supply supervisors for the stores allied with them. This attempt was not always successful. Many times former salesmen were designated as supervisors. As a rule they had neither the point of view, the information, nor the authority needed to do good jobs as supervisors. It was said that the chain-store supervisor gave instructions while the wholesalers' supervisors gave advice. Many independent retailers needed more than advice. However, over the years many retailer-owned and voluntary wholesalers have improved the quality of their supervisors, and many retailers have come to seek, respect, and use their advice.

Farm Problem

The prices of farm products have usually gone down more in periods of depression and up more in periods of prosperity than the prices of finished goods. The year 1920 was no exception, and the prices of farm products broke severely. The plight of the farmers was aggravated by the fact that many of them had bought land at boom prices. As farmers are widely distributed and vocal, they have more political power than their number would indicate. The period of the 1920's marks the beginning of the "farm problem." Remedies suggested in the 1920's were loans to tide farmers over the crisis; the growth of cooperative marketing organizations which it was hoped would reduce the cost of marketing and raise the price to the farmers; the increase in import tariffs on farm products; and subsidies by which the government would set up a corporation to purchase commodities and so maintain specified prices. The actual introduction of subsidies, however, remained until the following decade. Considerable progress was made in the establishment of farmers' cooperative marketing organizations. In this movement, the name of Aaron Sapiro, a California lawyer, should be mentioned. Sapiro was a very effective organizer, and there were a number of "Sapiro plan" cooperatives. The core of this plan was to have the farmers sign long-term (usually five years), legally binding contracts to market all of their products through the association, and the association on its side would provide a staff of experts to handle their business. It was felt by many that by cooperative marketing the farmers could secure monopoly prices. However, it was found that they were unable to control supply, and many of the cooperative organizations failed.

During the 1920's the prices of farm products increased slowly, and by the end of the decade it appeared that the situation would soon be improved sufficiently so that no additional legislation would be needed. This was prevented, however, by the severe depression of the early 1930's and a serious further drop in the prices of farm products.

Stable Price Theory

From the marketing viewpoint, there were a number of very interesting developments in this decade. One was the change in the popular theory of prices. During the period ending in 1920 there had been a very definite and strong feeling that prices were too high and that they should come down. They came down, and in 1922 they were roughly 50 percent above the prewar level. There was a widespread feeling that they should be stabilized. This probably came in part from the heavy losses in inventories in 1920. The idea of stable prices is an old one. As a boy I recall hearing a town loafer say: "Why do prices always have to change? Why don't we let the price of wheat be 75¢ a bushel, corn 50¢ a bushel, and meat at 10¢ a pound? These are fair prices and why don't we have them stay at these points?"

Judge Gary, who headed the United States Steel Corporation, argued that stable prices would stabilize business conditions. He felt that many of the ups and downs in business were caused by irregular buying—heavy buying on price increases and light buying on price declines. This theory became widespread. Professor

Irving Fisher* became its chief advocate and gave the theory respectability.† To those who believe that the free movement of price is the best regulator of business, this is a very vicious philosophy. Nevertheless it was widespread and had a great influence on the thinking of political and economic leaders and on economic conditions from 1922 to the present. There was considerable agitation during the 1920's to amend the Sherman antitrust law to permit price agreements among competitors. It was even alleged that some of the gangsters' activities were caused by the necessity of sellers resorting to violence to enforce and maintain uniform prices.

* Fisher was a professor at Yale University and a recognized leader in the fields of economics, money, and prices.
† It is the price level and not individual prices which is to be stabilized. However, it is doubtful if it is possible to stabilize the price level and have enough movement of prices of individual products to effectively adjust supply and demand. Sellers think of stabilization as applying to their individual products.

CHAPTER V

The 1930's—Desire for Security

Big Break, 1929–1932

Americans had a great deal of confidence in the 1920's. It was frequently said: "We have conquered the business cycle and will have no more depressions."* The basis of this feeling seems to have been the stability of prices and the belief that stable prices indicated a stable economy. (This fitted in with the widely quoted "profitless prosperity" slogan.)

In fact, Americans were having a boom without knowing it. Output per worker increased and prices remained stable (the average wholesale price index was the same for 1928 as for 1922), costs declined, and profits increased. The two reasons that seemed to have the greatest influence in explaining the break in 1929 were: (1) the end of the great highway-building era and (2) the failure of expenditures to keep pace with productive capacity of the nation. It was argued that if prices had been reduced, the consumers could have bought more goods and supported the economy and maintained employment. Other supports which could have worked (at least for a time) were continued expansion of the industrial plant, higher wages and salaries, or reduced hours of work. Failing any of these, the system collapsed.

Why were not prices reduced to keep pace with reduced costs of production? First, people had come to believe in stable prices; and second, they did not realize what was happening.

After the break started, why were not prices reduced as they

* This opinion was so widespread that Wesley C. Mitchell, of Columbia University and the National Bureau of Economic Research, and a leading authority on business cycles, felt called upon to issue a statement saying that "business cycles have not been ironed out and are likely to continue" (New York *Journal of Commerce*, April 15, 1929).

were in 1920? Again, it seems to have been the belief among manufacturers and merchants that stable prices were desirable and tended to stablize business conditions; and they naturally disliked going ahead and taking losses on inventories. There was also in the 1920's a desire for "cooperation" and a feeling against "cut-throat competition." This cooperation grew in part from the experiences during World War I when the government called businessmen together and encouraged their joint action in dealing with the government. Third, there were assurances from President Hoover that this was only a summer thunder shower and not a major storm. If businessmen would only keep spending, conditions would improve, and everything economic would be lovely. Public utilities including the railroads had planned to spend hundreds of millions of dollars in 1930 and they went ahead with their plans with the result that there was no sudden collapse in prices and business. The wholesale price index fell 3 percent from July to December 1929; 12 percent in 1930; and 12 percent in 1931. The total decline was 38 percent from July 1929 to February 1933. They were then at about the same level they had been during most of United States history except for the big war periods—Napoleonic wars and the War of 1812, Civil War, and World War I. Another thing well remembered was that the depression of 1920 had been short and it was expected that this depression would be short. There was no panic as there had been in some earlier depressions. Hence it seemed logical to expect this depression to be of short duration like those of 1907 and 1920. In the fall of 1931 when Colonel Ayers, a prominent business forecaster, said that the country was not nearly to the bottom, a wave of black despair spread over the country. By this time savings were pretty well exhausted, banks were closing their doors by the hundreds, and farm mortgages were being foreclosed by the thousands.

The break in prices of farm products was especially severe. Generally the prices of raw materials including farm products change more quickly and by greater percentages than do the prices of finished products. The average price of farm products dropped 59 percent from 1928 to 1932, while the price of finished products dropped only 27 percent.

Unemployment increased from an average of 429,000 in 1929 to 2,896,000 in 1930; 7,037,000 in 1931; 11,385,000 in 1932; and 11,842,000 in 1933.* Even so, there were more people employed than there were families. In 1930 the number of families (households) was approximately 30,000,000 and the number of persons employed was 46,000,000. In 1932 and 1933 there were nearly 39,000,000 people employed compared with perhaps 31,000,000 families. Unemployment could have been largely prevented by "spreading the work." Some private companies tried to do this by refusing to employ married women. This was by and large ineffective as only a part of private employers followed this policy and a husband could work for one company and his wife for another (the wife representing herself as being single if this were necessary to get a job). It would have taken firm action by the government to spread the jobs among families, and no such action was taken.

With so many people out of work and unable to find work, with savings exhausted, with mortgages being foreclosed on farms and homes, and with many people unable to borrow to build new homes or to buy appliances, there arose a great desire for security. In fact, the 1930's could be characterized by the desire for security. This idea was expressed by the young graduate who said: "I want security. I don't care if I never make much money. I would rather have a secure job at a small salary than a big salary in a position I might lose. I don't want to take the risk of starting my own business."

Why the change in sentiment compared with previous depressions? The country had gone through severe depressions in 1837, 1857, 1893, and 1920 without this big demand for security. Perhaps the difference was in the disappearance of available farm land. Up to 1893, the United States had been largely an agricultural nation. If one lost his job in the city, he could go back to the land. There was land available to buy or rent, or one could get a

* National Industrial Conference Board, Frederick W. Jones and Bess Kaplan (eds.), *The Economic Almanac, 1956* (New York: Thomas Y. Crowell Co., 1956).

job as a farmhand or work for a relative who had a farm. With the increase in urban population, disappearance of available farm land, and the use of farm machinery there was less and less of this opportunity to return to the land. Some did return to the farms in 1920–1921 but often with very disappointing results. Many got poor land. They lacked proper equipment and many lacked the needed skills. Many who lost their jobs and could find no others had to double up with relatives. It was not unusual to find two or three families living in one house. The unemployed started all kinds of makeshift businesses from running small stores, opening repair shops, to "selling apples on the street corners."

A second reason for the change in sentiment was the influence of the "New Deal" to be discussed a little later. The Democrats carried the election in 1932 on an economy platform. But shortly after coming into power, the Administration threw the economy platform out the window and inaugurated a program of "reform" and "recovery," both of which will be discussed later. No demand for such programs was evident, but the people were in a receptive frame of mind. They were in despair and welcomed any program that promised improvement.*

There was no "happy accident" to bring about recovery in the 1930's. No major industries or major new products came into general use. The 1920's saw the paving of highways, the sales of millions of automobiles, the introduction of the radio and mechanical home refrigerators, and a great increase in the use of many other appliances. In the 1930's came talking and colored moving pictures, but they represented no great increase in consumer expenditures. Theaters, hotel lobbies, restaurants, and some retail stores and railroad passenger cars were gradually air conditioned but this was not a major industry. Some railroads were buying

---

* A proposed panacea that attracted much attention temporarily was Technocracy. This promised earnings of $20 thousand a year for a few minutes of work a day. It called attention to the wonderful technological advances possible with machines and proposed a new political system operated by the technologists (chemists, physicists, engineers, biologists, and other scientists). Technocracy offered no practical plan of procedure, and interest died out as quickly in 1933 as it had arisen in 1931–1932.

diesel locomotives but much of this money would otherwise have gone for steam locomotives.* Freezer locker plants grew in number but they did not constitute a major industry. There was a large growth of rural electric lines. There were plenty of new products —paper bottles, quick-frozen foods, dry ice, nylon, steel houses, and many others, but none developed into a basic major industry during the decade. After touching bottom in the winter of 1932–1933 recovery was very slow, and this in spite of many government programs and heavy government expenditures.

Administered Prices

The failure of prices to come down enough to keep the economy operating at normal capacity, and to prevent unemployment during the late 1920's and the early 1930's, called attention to the fact that the economic system was not working the way it was supposed to work. Classical or orthodox economic theory had taught for a hundred and fifty years that when there was an oversupply of goods the sellers would reduce their prices until all the goods were sold. On the other hand, when there was a shortage of goods, the buyers would bid up the prices until the reduced demand at the higher prices equalled the supply. In this way the economic system was kept in balance. The beauty of this system was that it operated automatically and without the interferences of politicians and government bureaucrats. This theory was evolved, however, on the basis of a large number of relatively small producers and a large number of small consumers. This country never had conditions that permitted the system to work perfectly. There were always some monopolies established by the state, based on natural conditions, or secured more or less temporarily by combinations of shrewd traders. However, as long as the major portion of the

* The Pennsylvania Railroad electrified its lines from New York to Washington and Harrisburg largely with money borrowed from the government as a part of its "make-work" campaign. One wonders if this company would not have been better off if it had bought diesels in place of electric locomotives and saved the cost of electrification.

economy operated under relatively free competition, it worked reasonably well.

With the growth of the factory system, particularly in the metal trades, there were advantages to large plants, and many large companies came into existence. These large companies could control the market to their own advantage, or at least so they thought. Instead of lowering prices to keep the economy operating and labor employed, they produced only as much as they could sell at the prices which they themselves deemed to be "fair and reasonable." Then in the 1920's the theory of stable prices was used to assuage their consciences and make them feel righteous. The results of this course of action on the economy have been seen in the years 1928 to 1933. Economists who were in touch with business, and particularly marketing operations, had known the situation for some time. Market controls were described in reports of the Federal Trade Commission and the Department of Justice.

The failure of prices to come down as would "normally" have been expected in these years called attention forcibly to the changed competitive conditions. The 1930's saw studies pointing out that a few hundred corporations controlled a large proportion of the assets of all the business corporations. Books appeared on imperfect competition; monopolistic competition; concentration of the ownership of factories, banks, and public utilities; and competition between the few. Such words and phrases as "oligopoly," "duopoly," "administered prices," and "nonprice competition" came into use. There is, of course, competition between large companies because they want a larger share of the consumer's dollar. The consumer can spend his money in a variety of ways. (He can buy a new car or he can keep the old car and buy a radio, a fur coat, new furniture, a phonograph, a new furnace, or build another room to his house.) Thus different types of industries compete with each other. Manufacturers of similar goods may compete on quality, packages, service, or terms. While these may give the consumer more for his money, they are not substitutes for price competition.

It is said that many of the prices are now "administered." This means that they are not determined by the free play of competition. Administered prices are those set by individuals under imperfect or monopolistic competition and not by offers and bids on a free market.

The government (society) has not known what to do about the situation. Government has not intervened to break up the large corporations into enough smaller companies to restore keen price competition. The public believes that large companies can produce goods at lower costs than can small companies. The reduction in unit costs as volume increases is known as the "law of decreasing costs." However, this is a greatly overworked law. Studies have shown that in many industries medium-sized or small companies have lower unit costs than large companies. Nevertheless, the public seems to believe strongly in the advantages of large-scale production. Perhaps the greater advantage of the large company is in marketing—large advertising appropriations, extensive dealer organizations, ability to bargain for low buying prices, and ability to exert considerable control of selling prices. The large companies have created much public goodwill. For example, if one drives a General Motors car and gets much pleasure and good performance from it, he naturally has a friendly feeling for the General Motors Corporation.

The dilemma was obvious in the policy adopted towards the prices of farm products. There are large numbers of small producers. The prices of farm products have traditionally been determined on open and relatively free markets. The individual farmer can exert little influence on the price of his product—a fact which became painfully apparent in the early 1930's when most manufactured goods were sold under administered prices which did not respond to current conditions, and farm prices determined on a free market went down and down. The manufacturers maintained their prices, limited production to the quantities that could be sold at these prices, and laid off their workers. This reduced the ability of the workers to buy farm products and drove the farm prices still lower. The government, instead of restoring competition or forcing manufacturers to reduce their prices, elected to maintain artificially the prices of many farm products. The methods and expense of doing this are given elsewhere. The government is continuing to support the prices of farm products while allowing manufacturers to continue to "administer" their prices. If the country so strongly believes in the advantages of large companies that it allows them to exist, and if these companies continue to administer their prices on such an inflexible basis that the economy does not operate evenly, then the next step may logically be for the government to fix the selling prices of the large manufacturing companies as they do for the railroads and other public utilities. The danger of government price-fixing is that it would probably lead to less flexibility than now exists. The owners and managers of the large companies may wish that they had voluntarily divided their companies into smaller units, or that they had done a much better job of administering their prices.

Consumer Movement

Reduced incomes and the need for economy focused attention on the consumer and his problems. Consumers traditionally have had very little political influence. The groups with the most political power have been the farmers, the businessmen (manufacturers, railroads and other public utilities, bankers, and retailers), and the labor unions. Since people are all consumers, some thought that the consumers might come to have a considerable political power. Such was not the case. The movement expressed itself very largely in books, articles, lectures, and courses in schools and colleges. A book that had a very wide circulation was *Your Money's Worth* by Stuart Chase and F. J. Schlink. Its thesis was that the consumers were charged too much for many goods and that the solution would be to have goods sold by definite standards. Chase and Schlink felt that producers should be required to place the grade of the product on the product itself or the package and the consumers should be guided by this. It was argued that this would put competition on a price basis, where it belonged, and bring prices down.

There were also the so-called "horror" books describing the dangerous products—particularly drugs and foods—sold to the consumer. Typical examples of such books were *Chamber of Horrors* by Ruth Lamb, and *100,000,000 Guinea Pigs* by F. J. Schlink and Arthur Kallett.

A proposal was that the grade representing quality be indicated by A, B, or C, indicating first, second, or third quality, regardless of the product. It was feared that this would reduce the amount of advertising. Newpapers and other periodicals generally refused to publish anything relating to A-B-C labeling. This "campaign of silence" pretty well prevented the mass of consumers from learning much about the proposal. Whether or not the newspapers were responsible, no great popular demand arose for A-B-C labeling.

Two organizations—Consumers' Research and Consumers' Union—were formed to test goods and report the results to their subscribers. These have had a slow but a sizable growth, and both now have a considerable influence on consumers' purchasing.

Many excellent studies came out of this period. One of the best was *High Level Consumption* by William H. Lough and Martin R. Gainsbrugh, which was published in 1935. After a detailed analysis of the statistics of incomes and expenditures from 1909–1931, the prediction was made that if incomes continued to increase as they had during this period, the average family spending power in 1913 dollars would be $2,500 in the late 1940's. The authors did not foresee the long depression of the 1930's, and this income was not reached in the 1940's. The per family national income was very close to it in 1953, but the average family disposable income (income after taxes) is still considerably shy of the average of $2,500 in 1913 dollars ($7,100 in 1957 dollars).

The increasing family income meant that the family had more left after buying the necessities (food, clothing, shelter, and medical care) to spend in any way it saw fit. This came to be called "discretionary" buying power. Since the consumers can spend it in a variety of ways, it becomes more difficult to forecast the purchases of various goods and services. It becomes harder for the businessman to predict his sales and hence to plan his purchases and production. To meet this situation, the authors advocated more marketing research, and a new type of businessman and executive who was market and research minded. These recommendations have at least partly come true, as research has increased very rapidly and many of the business executives are market minded and research conscious. The authors also advocated smaller business concerns as they were thought to be more flexible and able more quickly to change their products and selling methods to meet changes in demand. There has been little or no trend toward smaller business concerns. The feeling in the 1950's is that the additional research of large concerns enables them to secure the desired flexibility.

Other notable books of the period were those of the Brookings Institution on production, consumption, income, and economic progress. The main thesis of these studies was that the advantages of increasing output should be passed on to the consumers in ever lower prices, so that all would benefit.

Declining Birth Rate

The birth rate in the United States, like that in western Europe, had been declining for some years. The death rate was also declining. The number of births per 1,000 population declined from 30 at the beginning of the century to 23.7 in 1920, to 18.9 in 1930, and to 17.9 in 1940. It was predicted that the birth rate would continue to decline to 11 per 1,000 in the next century. The proportion of old people in the population was increasing. The population of the United States was 106 million in 1920, 123 million in 1930, and 132 million in 1940. The population was increasing at a decreasing rate. It was predicted by the National Resources Board in 1938 that the population would reach a maximum of 158 million in 1980 and then start declining. A declining birth rate does not stimulate business. Families can live in smaller homes. Less furniture is needed. There is less need for children's clothes, toys, and schools. There were said to be one million empty seats in school houses in the late 1930's.

New Deal

Beginning in 1933 there was a period of increased government activity in the economic world. The activities of the government from 1933 to 1941 to stimulate, control, and regulate business and raise the scale of living for the people were covered by the term, "New Deal." There were too many of these activities (agencies, laws) to be described here. The best I can do is to characterize some of them briefly. There is a considerable difference of opinion as to their merit. They have been characterized as socialistic, useless, wasteful, harmful, foolish, expensive, communistic—and as delaying recovery on the one side and as the instruments of great social progress on the other. Regardless of which characterization is correct, they were definitely away from freedom and toward a controlled and regimented economy.

Things happen—how history would have been changed if some one event or act had been different is unknown but nevertheless furnishes interesting ground for speculation. Al Smith wanted very much to be President. McAdoo came to the 1924 Democratic convention with the most votes but the Smith group forced a deadlock from which John W. Davis emerged as a compromise or "dark horse" candidate. Smith was determined to have the Democratic nomination in 1928. The country was prosperous and there was little likelihood that the voters would change bosses and elect a Democrat. Some of Smith's opponents in the Democratic party said, "Let's nominate him and get rid of him." If Smith had been willing to wait until 1932 for the nomination, he likely would have been elected, for the country was then in the depths of a depression and it was highly improbable that the Republicans could have elected a candidate. If Smith had been elected in 1932, obviously things would have been different. He was a conservative, and it is safe to say that he would not have chosen many of the radical schemes that were adopted. No one knows whether this would have been better or worse. Many think that the country had reached the bottom and that business would have recovered as it had in all previous depressions—without more government bureaus, laws, deficits, and debts.

The banking moratorium of March 1933, and the reopening of the sound banks, restored confidence in the banks. This was generally hailed as a good and necessary action. Some think that it was the only action needed, and that if the administration had stopped there business recovery would have been quicker and sounder. However, the New Deal did not stop there.

National Recovery Administration

The National Recovery Administration was established in the summer of 1933 for two years on an experimental basis. The announced objective was the increasing of purchasing power. It was to be increased by raising wages. One is puzzled to know how purchasing power can be increased in this way. True, the man getting higher wages would have more purchasing power, but the man paying the higher wages would have less purchasing power, unless he raised the price of his product. If he raised his prices, this would reduce the purchasing power of his customers including the wage earners. However, higher wages were supposed to act as a "pump primer"—increased money income increases optimism and causes people to spend more freely. It is also argued that higher wages at the expense of employers' profits increases consumption expenditures at the expense of savings. Employers were exhorted not to raise their prices immediately since, if they did not, the increased purchasing power of the wage earners might be felt in the market before the impact of higher prices was fully effective.

The "deal" offered groups of businessmen when they came to Washington to negotiate NRA codes was to raise wages and agree to collective bargaining with labor unions in return for the privilege of raising prices through code provisions for fixing prices or for formulas for determining prices, open-price associations, outlawing unwanted competitive practices and the like. In brief, if businessmen would raise wages and agree to collective bargaining, they could limit competition and raise their prices.

Raising wages when there is widespread unemployment is a peculiar way of trying to increase employment. Higher wages encourage employers to introduce labor-saving machinery and to reorganize their work to reduce the number of workers. This was especially true in the late 1930's when money was available and interest rates were lower. It is difficult to raise prices when goods are plentiful, plants are running at a fraction of capacity, and purchasing power is limited. Many men agreed to the NRA codes in the belief that sales would increase for all, or that their competitors would adhere strictly to the code provisions while they could find loopholes that would enable them to increase their sales by underselling their competitors. A price agreement is a wonderful thing for an individual if his competitors hold to the agreed prices while he goes out and secretly cuts prices and increases his sales.

The code provisions very largely broke down of their own weight before the law was allowed to expire in 1935. One conviction for code violations that was widely published was that of the operator of a small pressing shop who pressed a pair of pants below the code price. Here was the mighty NRA in Washington which labored and fined a little pants presser for cutting his price ten cents! The constitutionality of the code provisions was tested in the Schechter or "sick chicken case," in which the Supreme Court decided that interstate commerce was not involved in the way chickens were taken out of a coop. The federal government was therefore without authority to regulate local marketing practices.

The Brookings Institution made a rather lengthy and detailed study of the NRA and came to the conclusion that it definitely delayed and hampered recovery. However, it made no attempt to evaluate its operations as an instrument of social reform.

Prices in mid-1933 were at about the average level of "normal" or peacetime prices throughout this country's history. Why then should it have been a major objective of the government to raise them?* Perhaps it goes back to the belief that the prices of the 1920's were the "just and fair" prices.

"Boondoggling"

The various "make-work" agencies—PWA, WPA, NYA, and CCC—brought into common use the term "boondoggling" or doing unneeded or little needed things and doing them very slowly. The feeling that many of the projects were "make-work" and of rela-

* President Roosevelt in a national radio address said that prices would be restored to their 1926 level and never again allowed to fluctuate.

tively little value spread among the workers so that they loafed at their jobs. This may be illustrated by two students who were hired under a make-work program and put to washing windows. One boy said, "We have already washed that window." The other replied, "You don't have the spirit of this job. It doesn't make any difference if we have washed the window, we can wash it many more times. Our object is to make this job last as long as we can, so they don't run out of jobs for us to do." In spite of much wasted effort, some worthwhile things were done, such as building and repairing roads, developing parks, and building and repairing school houses. However, prosperity cannot be increased by boondoggling production of little-needed goods and services. Prosperity is based on production of useful things.

Farm Aid

From 1921 to 1929 various kinds of aid for the farmers were tried or proposed. One was lending money to the farmers at favorable interest rates and getting them deeper into debt. Will Rogers remarked that getting the farmers deeper in debt was a peculiar form of "relief." These loans were made in the belief that the low prices of farm products were temporary and that loans would tide the farmers over until prices rose. This proved to be partly true and prices of farm products were getting back into line with other prices when the 1929 depression started. Several factors slowed up this adjustment. Tractors were being substituted for horses, and tractors do not eat hay and oats. Many European countries were limiting imports. The acreage in this country had been expanded during the war years, 1916–1919, and farmers were slow in taking this acreage out of cultivation.

Cooperative marketing of farm products was encouraged and marketing organizations increased in number and volume of business. It was believed that they could reduce marketing costs and that the reduction would revert to the farmers as higher prices. Many believed that they could secure control of supplies and get monopoly prices. In the latter belief they were mistaken as they did not succeed in controlling supplies for any great length of time.

Some cooperative associations failed but many succeeded and apparently helped their members. It was said of some of the failures: "They succeeded," meaning that they forced the private marketing agencies to reduce their margins and raise their prices to the farmers; but the cooperative could not operate on the lower margins.

Tariffs were increased on some farm products. Such increases could only be effective on products which were imported.

Subsidies were proposed but rejected because, if the price were raised, farmers would increase supplies and place an ever-increasing burden on the taxpayers.

The Federal Farm Board was established in 1929 with a capital of $500 million. Its object was to purchase surplus farm products and so support prices. The goods purchased were to be held until they could be resold at a profit, or exported, if necessary, at a loss. But for the depression starting in 1929 the Farm Board might have met with success. However, it was soon realized that the prices of farm products could not be supported at profitable levels unless the farmers reduced the supply. They were asked to do so, but it was hard for them to do so individually. If one reduced his acreage, others might increase their acreages. The net result of the operations of the Farm Board was to slow up the decline in prices until its $500 million was exhausted.

Farm prices dropped drastically. At the low point in the winter of 1932–1933 farmers in the corn belt received ten cents to twelve cents a bushel for their corn. There was, however, little unemployment among the farmers. In fact, the income of farmers dropped little, if any, more than the income of industrial workers. The difference was that the income of all farmers declined. The wage rates of industrial workers dropped much less but many were unemployed and so had no wages. The money income of farmers and of industrial workers (railroad payrolls, factory payrolls, and construction payrolls) moved closely together from 1921 through 1932. Considering the farmer's living from the farm, his real income perhaps dropped less than that of the industrial worker's. At the bottom of the depression, a farmer said: "But we eat just as good as we ever did."

The aggravating fact was that the prices of many things the

farmers bought, such as farm implements, dropped much less than the price of things the farmers sold. The difference was that the farmer maintained production and sold his products on a free market for what they would bring. On the other hand, many manufacturers followed the theory of maintained and stable prices and elected to close their plants and lay off workers rather than keep up production and let supply and demand determine prices. Manufacturers could have sold at auction and ascertained prices on a free market (as Alexander Smith & Company did at times with its carpets and rugs) and then, if necessary, adjust their costs, including wages, downward. Generally, workers would be better off working at somewhat lower wages than not working at all, and under the prevailing conditions they would have been willing to do so. In fact, many factories closed or reduced their operations, reduced payrolls, and so reduced the demand for—and hence the prices of—farm products. The farmer was thus in effect made to bear much more than his share of maintaining the economic system. In my opinion, the farmers deserved relief (preferably from increased output and lower prices of manufactured goods). They had the political power to get relief whether or not they deserved it.

It was obvious that if farm prices were to be raised some limitations had to be placed on supply until domestic demand could catch up or until foreign demand was found. Voluntarily the farmers failed to reduce supplies. Several plans had been suggested. The one adopted was contained in the Agricultural Adjustment Act of May 12, 1933. Under this plan the farmers were paid for reducing their acreages of certain crops and their breeding of hogs. Acreages were to be increased or decreased in accordance with estimated needs. The acreage allotments were broken down by states, counties, townships, and individual farms. If the farmer did not sign up to reduce his acreage he received no pay. In 1933 this plan involved plowing up some planted crops and killing some pigs. This action was greatly criticized by city and farm people alike. It seemed unreasonable to a person who was having a hard time getting enough to eat to read about food being wantonly destroyed. The money to pay the farmers was to come from a processing tax on the products and was to be passed on to the consumers like a sales tax. The Supreme Court declared this tax unconstitutional. Congress then provided that the cost be paid from the general funds in the Treasury—that is, from taxes.

The Agricultural Adjustment Act of 1938, among other things, provided for payments to the farmers for soil conservation. The top foot of soil is the most important resource in the world. Without it, the human race would die of starvation. However, it seems a rather far-fetched function of government to pay a man for saving his own property. It would seem that an enlarged educational program for conservation would accomplish the results desired. If more drastic action were needed, why not condemn the farms of those wasting the soil and resell them to people who would conserve the soil?

If the payments to the farmers for reducing supply had been used only during the depression years of the early and middle 1930's, little criticism would be needed—the payments were an emergency measure and after serving the immediate purpose they should have been discontinued. However, they were not discontinued. They were retained during World War II and through the postwar boom when prices were high and farmers were asked to increase production. Farmers remain divided on the desirability of retaining price supports, and those who want supports disagree on how much is needed. Payments to the farmers under the various "adjustment" acts have amounted to some ten billion dollars. Less than one-third of this was paid during the 1930's, the emergency period in which payments were needed to give the farmers time to adjust their operations to the changed conditions.

Farm production has been increased during the past eighteen years by hybrid seeds, better feeding of livestock, improved methods of dry farming in the West, soil conservation, and favorable weather.

Other Programs

The devaluation of the dollar gave export trade an immediate stimulus and increased employment temporarily.

The Reconstruction Finance Corporation, started in the 1920's, seemed highly desirable in providing money to private companies which needed cash for recovery and expansion programs.

"Social Security," including the system of old age pensions, has proven a popular program but is seriously criticized as being unwise and unsound. Much can be said for old age pensions for all persons. Under the U. S. system of government it would appear that such pensions should be provided by the private companies or the states and not by the federal government. There is also much to be said in favor of annuities or pensions for everyone on a voluntary basis. It is, however, undemocratic to make such pensions compulsory. If individuals are too improvident to provide old age pensions for themselves, it can be argued that they should be allowed to take their chances with "relief" or an old age pension provided free. The adverse criticisms of social security are that the costs are inequitably assessed; that many people have and will get pensions that they do not earn; and that the system is compulsory, forcing many individuals and groups to take these pensions when they do not want them. It is difficult to justify such action in a democracy. This is benevolent autocracy with a will.

Legislation Against Price Cutting

In the mid-1930's laws were passed by forty-five states allowing sellers to fix the prices at which their customers would resell their branded goods—resale-price maintenance (the so-called "fair trade" laws). Congress passed a law legalizing this practice between states having resale-price maintenance laws. Many small retailers (particularly retail druggists) had advocated such laws hoping to prevent chain and cut-price stores from underselling them. Before the passing of these laws, manufacturers could maintain the resale prices of their goods by consigning them to the dealers, and they could, in the majority of cases, control the resale prices by refusing to sell to the price cutters or to the wholesalers who sold to price cutters. The first new laws legalized contracts for resale-price maintenance. Many buyers would not sign the contracts. So laws were passed binding nonsigners to contracts signed by other buyers in their state. Very much to the surprise of even many of the advocates, the United States Supreme Court upheld these laws. However, the legality of such provisions is again in question at this writing and several of the state courts have ruled out the provision binding nonsigners.

Robinson-Patman Amendment

Perhaps of greater importance was the Robinson-Patman amendment to the Clayton antitrust act passed in 1936. One of its main objectives was to reduce or abolish the buying advantages which the chains had over the independents. The small retailers felt that a considerable part of the ability of the chains to undersell them came from their lower buying prices. Perhaps the most active group in lobbying the bill through Congress was comprised of the food brokers who did not like the chains bypassing them and buying directly from the manufacturers.

The central idea of the Robinson-Patman amendment was that a manufacturer or processor should sell to all competing retailers or to all competing wholesalers at the same price except as the larger quantities purchased or a reduction in the services rendered to a buyer justified a lower price to him than to his competitor. Many chains operate wholesale houses and perform the wholesale functions of storing, dividing, selling, and delivering the goods to their own retail stores. In such cases, the chains are entitled to the same prices as are the wholesalers. The larger chains buy in larger quantities than do most of the independent wholesalers. This may entitle them to lower prices than given the wholesalers. In the 1920's and the 1930's the chain-store wholesale warehouse commonly operated at lower expense than did the independent wholesaler. The chain required its retail store managers to requisition the goods from the warehouse while the wholesaler sent his salesmen to the retailers to solicit their business. The chain-store warehouse delivered goods to the retail stores on a definite schedule. Staple groceries were usually delivered once a week. The trucks could thus go out fully loaded and make only a limited number of stops for unloading. In contrast, the independent wholesaler, in order to hold his customers, often had to make numerous small deliveries to his retailer customers. In these and other ways, the chain-store warehouse often had lower operating expenses than did the independent wholesaler.

To meet this competition, many wholesalers have adopted many of the chain methods, dispensing with their salesmen and requiring the retailers to write out and mail in their orders, and to receive goods on specified days. In this way, many wholesalers have laid goods down in retail stores at a price competitive with the cost of the chains in delivering goods to their retail stores. Many independent retailers have adopted self-serve—cash-carry methods of operation, thus getting their expenses down to a point where they are competitive with the chains.

It has been the changed methods and increased efficiency of operation and not legislation that have enabled the independent retailers to stay in business and compete with the chains. The Robinson-Patman amendment in some cases has helped and in some cases has hurt the independent retailers. It has helped in forcing the manufacturers to make available to them advertising and other allowances available to buyers of large quantities. On the other hand, it has hurt the independents by preventing voluntary wholesalers from receiving brokerage rebates which were passed along to the retailers in lower prices.

An over-all evaluation of the operation of the Robinson-Patman amendment is difficult. There are apparently smaller differences in prices between large and small buyers than there were prior to 1936. It is, however, difficult to determine how much influence the Robinson-Patman amendment had on evening up prices and how much came from market conditions (seller's market) that enabled sellers to make sales without large price concessions. Advertising allowances have been made available to smaller buyers. The general opinion seems to be that the Robinson-Patman amendment has made for better and healthier competition by helping the smaller buyers. On the other side critics contend that it has made for "weak" competition—that it has, in fact, weakened rather than strengthened competition.

It is interesting that the decade of the 1930's saw laws passed seeking protection for the independent retailers against the competition of the chains while requests for protective laws had failed against the department stores in the 1890's and against the mail-order houses in the 1900's. The city retailers opposed the department stores, and the rural retailers opposed the mail-order houses, while both city and rural retailers opposed the chains. The passage of the antichain-store laws may also indicate a growing belief in government regulation of business activities.

Supermarkets

The rise of the supermarkets was the most spectacular single marketing development of the 1930's. They appeared in the early 1930's in several eastern industrial cities at about the same time. Securing vacant buildings, buying distress goods and advertising them vigorously at low prices, they quickly attracted crowds of buyers. The consumers were short of money. The fact that the goods were displayed in warehouse buildings which were outside of established shopping centers was only a minor deterrent. In fact, the availability of parking space may have been an advantage. The supermarkets were an almost instantaneous success and grew so rapidly that in five years they were fully established throughout the country. There were at first several types: Some operators leased many of the departments. Some had only the very cheapest fixtures. On the other hand, some soon obtained nice buildings and put in expensive fixtures. There was, in the late 1930's, considerable discussion as to which type of market would win—the warehouse type with cheap fixtures, or the one in an attractive building and expensive and elaborate fixtures. A few predicted that they would evolve into a new type of department store located outside the shopping district and handling a variety of goods including clothing. Markets of the "warehouse" type soon were in the majority. Some supermarkets have buildings that are little more than sheds and some have nice brick, steel, and concrete buildings with neat fixtures. Those with luxurious fixtures are in the minority. Leased departments have decreased in importance.

The supermarket was popularly hailed as a radically different and new kind of store. Rather, it was the result of evolution but its entrance was hastened by the large quantities of low-priced goods, vacant buildings available at low rent, and the reduced income of the consumers in the middle 1930's. The self-serve—cash-carry method of operation was already well established and widely used.

Grocery stores became larger and grew into full-fledged food stores handling groceries, meats, produce, bakery goods, and dairy products. The chains were finding their small neighborhood stores expensive to supervise, and especially with the higher wage rates of the 1920's, many small stores were becoming unprofitable. With automobiles in general use, cash-carry stores no longer had to be in the residential neighborhoods. Housewives could take the goods home in their cars. If the husband used the car to drive to work, he could stop for groceries on his way home, or husband and wife could shop together in the evening. Hence demand developed for stores open in the evenings, and, during World War II, with factories working around the clock, some supermarkets remained open twenty-four hours a day.

The supermarket was a logical development of existing trends. Some "warehouse-type" stores had been tried out in the 1920's and had operated at low expenses (6–10 percent). Plans for larger stores operated on the self-serve–cash-carry method located outside the downtown shopping district where parking space was available were being evolved in the minds of alert grocery operators in the 1929–1931 period. Reduced family incomes in the early 1930's made the supermarket a "natural." The large volume of business gave the independent retailer buying power enough to enable him to compete with the chains, and many of the early supermarkets were started by independents. Some of the chains were slow to open supermarkets. They were making satisfactory profits, and it is natural for such concerns to be cautious in adopting new methods. Some chains suffered a large decline in sales and severe reductions in profits before getting wholeheartedly into the supermarket business.

Some point out that a predecessor of the supermarket had developed in Los Angeles. A typical arrangement of this type of market consisted of shops on two sides of a lot with the other two sides being available for parking. The market might contain several small shops selling groceries, fruits, meats, bakery goods, drugs, flowers, variety goods. This was a neighborhood shopping center for convenience goods providing a limited amount of parking space.

It differed from the supermarkets in not having a large store with mass displays of goods.

The supermarket continued to develop in the 1940's and the 1950's. They have continued to broaden their lines and increase in size. A supermarket with sales of $10 thousand a week or $500 thousand a year appears to be large enough to operate efficiently, but stores with sales of $40 thousand a week or $2 million a year are common, while there are some with sales of $5 million and of $10 million a year. Many supers have added drugs, toilet articles, cosmetics, housewares, hosiery, house and work clothing, phonograph records, magazines, stock feeds. Such lines have been added to increase sales or to increase the percentage of gross margin as some of these lines carry higher margins than groceries.

A new type of jobber, the rack jobber, came into existence to supply food stores with nonfood lines such as drugs and housewares. The rack jobber supplies shelves or racks (hence the name) on which he displays his wares. He keeps the racks stocked and collects from the market operator for the goods sold. These jobbers are very helpful in supplying lines with sales too small to justify the employment of buyers and display men by the market operator. Some large operators prefer to buy from jobbers to building their own merchandising organizations to handle minor lines such as drugs, toilet articles, household hardware, or housewares.

Some supermarkets are successful without providing parking space. This may be true in an apartment house district where there are enough customers within carrying distance, say a radius of four blocks; or in smaller towns where there is parking space in the streets. The trend, however, is to provide more parking space. Early markets provided one square foot of parking space to one square foot of store space. This ratio increased to as much as two or three times as much parking space as space in the store. At this writing the supermarkets like to have a ratio of at least four to one.

The developments of chain stores and supermarkets resulted in cutting in half the cost of distributing groceries from the manufacturers to the consumers. Prior to the rapid development of chain stores in the 1920's, typical expenses of wholesale grocers were 10 percent; and typical gross margins, including profits, 12 percent.

Typical expenses of retail grocers were 17 percent; and typical gross margins, 18.5 to 19 percent. An item selling to the wholesale grocer at $1.00 would be sold to the retailer at $1.14 to allow a margin of 12 percent on selling price. This item would be sold to the consumer at $1.40 to allow a 19 percent margin to the retailer. The typical supermarket gross margin is some 16 or 17 percent, so that an article sold by the manufacturer for $1.00 would reach the consumer at $1.20 (allowing 16.7 percent on selling price). The old margin was forty cents; the new one, twenty cents. Many independent retailers have been able to meet the supermarket price by changing to self-service and buying from retailer-owned or voluntary wholesalers which operate at substantially the same expense as the chain-store warehouses. Other independents operate on a service basis, extending credit and making deliveries; selecting locations close to the consumers; or by keeping longer hours than the chain stores.

Branch Stores

During the 1920's and the 1930's, cities spread out more and more into suburbs, a movement stimulated by the automobile. Branch stores increased in number. The branch store is controlled and merchandised from the parent store, while the chain store is merchandised from a common center. Branch stores continued to develop during the 1940's and the 1950's. Considerable economy is possible with branch stores, as one set of buyers can buy for the main store and its branches, and, if the branches are located in one metropolitan area, one advertisement can be used to cover the goods for sale in all stores.

Motor Truck Transportation

The 1930's saw a rapid increase in the intercity movement of goods by truck. A network of surfaced roads had been built. The truck had been improved and put on pneumatic tires. Larger trucks were built and the tractor-trailer developed. There was unemployment, and drivers could be obtained at relatively low wages as compared to the wage rates paid by the railroads. (Fifty cents an hour was a common wage in the early 1930's.) If a man could buy, rent, or borrow a new or used truck, he could go into business for himself. If near a coal mine, he could buy coal and sell it to the household consumers in surrounding towns. He could buy produce from farmers and haul it to nearby or distant towns and sell to the retailers or to the consumers. Many operators reinvested their earnings in additional trucks and came to operate fleets of trucks. Laws were passed regulating the operation of trucks, especially of common carrier trucks—those holding themselves to carry goods for the public at established rates. As the industry became organized, tariffs, similar to those of the railroads, were developed and filed with public service commissions listing the rates charged between various cities.

The truck has several advantages over the railroad in that it often shortens trade channels, reduces handling and packing expense, and reduces the time required for delivery of the goods. For example, if a trucker buys goods from a farmer and sells to city retailers, he substitutes one haul for three or four hauls and eliminates two or three middlemen. If the goods are shipped by rail, they have to be loaded at the farm, hauled to the local railroad station, loaded on the freight car, moved to the city, unloaded on the platform of the wholesaler, loaded on a truck and hauled to the retail store. If the wholeslae receiver is not also a jobber, another haul to the jobber's store is involved. If the trucker buys from the farmer and sells to the retailer, he thus bypasses the country buyer and the wholesale receiver. As trucking developed, it was found to save time for the trucker to buy at a country assembling market (from the grower, a commission man, country buyer, or auctioneer). He then often sells to the city jobber. In this case, he bypasses the city wholesale market and saves several handling expenses.

Packing and crating expenses are often less on truck than on rail hauls. This is an especially important advantage in shipping household goods.

The reduction in time is another important advantage in truck shipments. A wholesale warehouse, for example, loads the trucks during the day, and they are moved at night reaching retail stores located in a radius of two or three hundred miles early the next morning. Less-than-carload rail shipments would require from two to ten days to reach these same destinations. The saving of time is so important in shipping livestock, for example, that many central markets receive little or no stock by rail.

In spite of their advantages, the trucks come in for much criticism for congesting traffic on streets and highways, and also for not paying their fair share of building and maintaining the roads. Taxes and license fees for trucks have been increasing. It is felt that many trucks are too heavy and too large; and also it is felt that with the more powerful diesel engines they move at speeds too high for the good of the highways.

The intercity movement of goods by trucks has increased until it is estimated that they move one-fourth as many ton miles as do the railroads.*

Recession and Recovery

By the end of 1936 the general belief was that business was definitely on the upswing and that the depression would soon be over. Unemployment had dropped 40 percent from its peak. National income had risen from $42 billion in 1933 to $65 billion in 1936, or 44 percent. Wholesale prices rose 23 percent. Allowing for the increase in consumer prices, the per capita national income rose 28 percent. Forecasts at the beginning of 1937 were almost universally optimistic—there were no clouds in the sky, and business was going to be good for many years. In August of 1937 came the much discussed "recession." The government would not admit that it was another depression and so characterized it as a "recession." In anticipation of higher prices, businesses had stocked up on goods. Sales were good and prices were rising. However, all the goods were not moving into consumption. Many were going into inventories. When the warehouses were full, purchasing de-

* When all local movements are considered—pickup and delivery, to and from rail terminals; movement between warehouses, stores, and factories— the truck moves (*i.e.*, originates) several times as many goods as do the railroads.

clined, men were laid off, prices broke, and inventory losses amounted to many millions of dollars.

To help prevent a recurrence of this situation, the United States Department of Commerce began gathering figures on wholesale and retail inventories. The availability of inventory data presumably enables businessmen to guard against building their inventories too high—at least they have information as to the facts.

Employment dropped by four million from July to December 1937 and early in 1938 there were eleven and a half million unemployed. There was little improvement in employment until the summer of 1940 when the defense program started and war orders were received from Europe. National income went up in 1940 and very rapidly in 1941 when the U. S. defense program increased. Unemployment was down to three and a half million by December 1941. Such facts form the basis for the statement that it took a war to get the country out of the depression.

Evaluation

Per capita disposable income adjusted for price changes was the same in 1939 as in 1929. In other words there was no increase in "real" per capita income during the decade. In other decades having depressions, there were increases in per capita income. There was a severe depression in 1873; yet the per capita income adjusted for price changes was 30 percent higher in 1879 than in 1869. A severe degression started in 1893; yet the per capita income was 20 percent higher in 1899 than in 1889. There was some 14 percent increase in the per capita income in 1909 over 1899, in spite of the depression of 1907. During the decade of the 1920's, the per capita real income increased some 5 percent in spite of the depression, and in spite of the fact that the increase was measured from the boom year of 1919. In spite of a recession in 1949, per capita real income was 38 percent over that of 1939.

This would lead to the conclusion that all the New Deal laws, bureaus, commissions, and policies hindered rather than helped the economy. A claim made by friends of the New Deal was that it fostered social progress by bringing about a more even distribution of income—that it helped the poor at the expense of the rich. This was not the case. The following are estimates of the distribution of income by families:

Family income	1929 Brookings Institution estimate (percentage)	1939 Macfadden Publication estimate (percentage)
Under $1,000	21.5	32
$1,000–$1,999	38.0	37
$2,000–$2,999	19.0	19
$3,000–$4,999	13.5	8
$5,000 and over	8.0	4
	100.0	100

The percentage of families in the low income groups increased between 1929 and 1939. The cost of living, however, was 17 percent lower in 1939 than in 1929. Even allowing for the lower living cost, a higher proportion of the families were in lower income brackets in 1939 than in 1929.

Probably the most popular "reform" of the New Deal was the introduction of a government-operated compulsory old age pension system, commonly referred to as Social Security. Some would say that the fostering of labor unions was another important "reform." The NRA, Wagner, and other legislation forced labor unions on many employers who did not want them. The unions obviously did the workers as a whole little or no good in the 1930's, but it is argued that the unions formed in this decade grew and later in the next decade became very important and very helpful to workers.

In the middle and late 1930's it was said that the man with a job was better off than he had ever been, for his wages had risen much faster than the cost of living and he had a retirement pension, vacation with pay, sick benefits, and increased job security. On the other hand, the man without a job was worse off than at any time in the history of this country for he had less chance of getting a job. Labor legislation, government boards, and labor unions evidently helped some people at the expense of others.

The value of unions to their members, to workers who are not members, to employers, to sellers of goods, and to society is much debated. There are many arguments that the unions are of great benefit to their members and other arguments that their real wages would be just as high and working conditions just as good without them. To explore and weigh these arguments would take this discussion too far afield. However, one observation seems warranted, that the union officers are among the leading advocates of inflation, arguing for ever higher wages which make for higher prices. For a long-term policy to benefit their members and society, it might be better to try to maintain present wage rates and advocate lower prices. This would increase real wages. It was pointed out above that the big business barons of fifty years ago were so newly arrived that they did not realize the social responsibility of big business. Just so, it appears today that the leaders of "Big Labor" do not fully realize and appreciate that their positions carry heavy social responsibilities.

During the 1930's there was a definite loss of personal freedom. Businessmen have had more laws to obey, more reports to make, more taxes to pay; members of labor unions now have more orders and rules to obey, have two bosses, and are often limited in changing jobs by loss of seniority rights; farmers have come to have more rules to follow and reports to make in obeying the various acreage quotas; citizens in general have come to have to keep more records and pay more taxes. One group definitely benefited has been the accountants.

Economic Power and the Residual Theory

It has been said that the strongest group in society gets the best "deal" and the weakest group gets the poorest "deal," or the "residue" of the national income. At one time the strongest group may be the landowners; at another time, the military; at another time, the priesthood; at another time, the laborers. In the United States at the opening of the century, the bankers, the railroad operators, and the manufacturers made up the strongest group. The railroads lost their ascendancy in the 1900's with the regulations of the Interstate Commerce Commission and other regulatory bodies, and the increasing costs of operation. They were squeezed on one side by regulatory commissions and on the other by the labor unions (brotherhoods). The bankers lost power with the operations of the Federal Reserve System, the Security and Exchange Commission, the various government agencies for loaning to the farmers, and the Reconstruction Finance Corporation. The manufacturers are still in a relatively strong position but have seen the rise of countervailing power in the growth of large retailers—for example, Sears, Roebuck & Company and the Great Atlantic and Pacific Tea Company; in the growth of labor unions; and in the passage of the Robinson-Patman amendment to limit their freedom in price making. The labor unions have had a great increase in power during the past two decades and are now one of the more powerful groups in the economy. Judging by the history of the past fifty years they may expect to have their power limited and controlled by government regulation.*

With power comes responsibility. In the American system if those with power do not accept the responsibility that goes with it, sooner or later they will see their power curtailed. This may come from government regulation, the rise of countervailing power, or the loss of market to new or substitute products. Wages are the price of labor. If prices should be flexible, so should wages. As wages have traditionally followed prices up or down, workers would not be injured on a downswing. They might, in fact, be much benefited if reduced costs kept the products moving into consumption and plants operating.

* The farmer is too small individually to have any noticeable economic power. The farmers, however, as a group have much greater political power than would be indicated by their number, because of their distribution. Each state has two senators, which gives the rural states a large representation in the Senate. Many small and medium-sized cities are situated in congressional districts that are largely rural. In such districts the Congressmen are particularly conscious of the "farm vote."

CHAPTER VI

World War II

The year 1942 saw increased expenditures for defense and the United States entry into the war in December. The nation had the immediate problem of switching to a war economy. Production of war goods had to be increased and civilian goods curtailed. Millions of fighting men had to be trained and equipped. Other workers had to take their jobs. Prices had to be regulated. Consumption patterns had to be altered.

There was a "miracle of production." The physical volume of goods manufactured more than doubled, the physical volume of farm products marketed increased more than 25 percent, and the physical volume of minerals produced increased more than 30 percent. This was done with some ten million of the country's strong young men under arms. Their places were taken by women, younger and older men, and by men previously unemployed, many of them formerly submarginal as workers. Considering these facts, the record of producing goods for the armed forces, for the forces of the nation's allies, and for civilian populations was really a miracle.

There was an equally great miracle of distribution. The raw materials, as well as the finished products, had to be transported to the armies and to civilian markets. The railroads practically broke down under their job in World War I while in World War II they did their job so well that there was no talk of government operation. Ships were built and transported many of the goods overseas. Goods had to be sold to munitions makers, to other manufacturers, to distributors, to the government, and to the consumers. There were fewer occupational deferments in the distributive than in other trades. Yet the job was done. The civilian per capita consumption of some nondurable goods, like foods, increased. Durable goods were often unobtainable, so many consumers increased their purchases of the available nondurable goods.

Price Controls

The United States learned much about price controls in World War I. When the United States entered World War II, the country had this experience, two years of experience by England and Canada, and the experience of Germany under National Socialism for guides. The bulk-line principle used in World War I leads to high prices as prices are set high enough to allow many high-cost producers to operate without a loss. Cost-plus prices are wasteful as the producer is allowed a price that covers his cost plus a profit. If his cost increases his profit is larger. Hence the attempt was made to avoid these methods, although both were used at times, especially the cost-plus contract in government purchases.

Consumer incomes went up. More people were employed. Rising wages and overtime payments increased the earnings of workers greatly. For example, many factory workers had their earnings increased from $30 to $100 a week. The earnings of businessmen increased. National dollar income increased 25 percent in 1941 over 1940 and continued to increase rapidly, personal incomes being 80 percent higher in 1945 than in 1941. Incomes were larger than the available goods, the difference being called the "inflationary gap." To close this gap, higher taxes were advocated, people were encouraged to save, especially by the purchase of government bonds, and credit purchases were discouraged. Most economists advocated higher taxes than were levied.

Beginning in 1940, industry was asked to limit price advances, especially on basic raw materials, and the procurement divisions of the Army and Navy were asked not to bid against each other and so raise prices. In 1941 the Office of Price Administration set maximum price schedules and depended upon publicity and voluntary cooperation for compliance. This resembled—but was much less vocal than—decrying the profiteers in World War I. After the passage of the Emergency Price Control Act in January 1942, a "price freeze" was put into effect in April, setting the prices charged by manufacturers and merchants in March as their maximum prices. Provisions were made for relief in exceptional cases. On the whole, this was effective, at least temporarily. As cost advanced, producers and merchants needed higher prices. Then formulas for determining prices were established using wage rates, material costs, and overhead costs. In many cases, specific prices were set, using the bulk-line formulas in some instances. Cost-plus contracts were numerous in government purchases and contracts. In many cases, construction had to be started before the costs were known. This was frequently true in the building of newly designed equipment such as planes, tanks, and ships.

To make supplies go around, numerous products were rationed, notably some foods and gasoline.

On the whole, price controls were effective. Wholesale prices advanced some 13 percent from 1939 to 1941. During the war from 1941 to 1945 prices advanced only 21 percent. The total advance from 1939 to 1945 was some 37 percent.

Postwar Inflation

Most price controls were rescinded in 1946. Many argued that they should be retained for a longer time. On the other side it was felt that many government "bureaucrats" wanted to keep price controls permanently and that to prevent this they should be repealed before a permanent organization was set up. It was also remembered that the price boom after World War I had been very short. Prices rose rapidly, going up 46 percent from 1945 to 1949. It can be argued on one side that the wartime controls only delayed price advances which were inevitable; and on the other that if price controls had been continued until production had had a chance to catch up with demand, price advances would have been substantially less.

There was a pent up demand for goods. Automobiles had not been produced during the war years and many of the old cars needed replacement. Many men getting out of the service wanted cars. The same was true of many other durable goods. Young married couples wanted houses and furniture. Factories had to convert to civilian goods. It took considerable time for supplies to catch up with demand. Price controls might have helped considerably for a time. However, blackmarketing had been increasing. It is questionable as to how long it could have been held sufficiently in check to allow price controls to be effective.

CHAPTER VII

1946–1959—Gadget Economy

It has been hard for me to realize and grasp the significance of the fact that the United States emerged from World War II as one of the two great powers in the world. The United States is not prepared for world leadership—just as no nation in history has ever been prepared or qualified for world leadership. This country tries to lead the world toward democracy and against autocracy. Posterity will have to judge how wisely or how foolishly this leadership has been used.

Population

A most startling fact has been the increase in the birth rate. It has astounded the prophets. It rose slightly in 1941, increasing from 17.9 in 1940 to 18.8 in 1941. In 1943 it increased to 21.5. After the close of the war, it went up sharply to 23.3 in 1946, and to 24.6 in 1952, and up again in 1954 to 25—beyond the rate prevailing in 1916. It was generally thought that the declining birth rate is linked with the prosperity of the country, that when incomes are low in relation to their standard of living people reduce the size of their families. As the death rate has declined, it has required fewer births to keep up the population. On this basis it is predicted that when incomes again decline the birth rate will also decline. Some believe that war causes people to feel that they should have more children to protect the country. Still others feel that there has been a fundamental change in the philosophy or mores of the people in regard to families.

The population of the country increased from 139 million in 1945 to 171 million in 1957. Aided by the increased birth rate, lowered death rate, and immigration, the population has already passed the 158 million maximum that it was predicted in the 1930's would be reached in 1980.

From a marketing point of view, the increasing birth rate was of great importance. It meant a demand for more children's clothes, more toys, larger houses, suburban homes, more furniture, more schools, and more educational equipment of all kinds.

There have been many geographical shifts in population both during and after World War II. There has been a continuing shift from the farm to the city. With the increased use of farm machinery, fewer workers are needed on the farms. Farm population declined relatively—from 35 percent of the total in 1910 to 25 percent in 1928, to 20 percent in 1943, to 16 percent in 1952, and to 12.5 percent in 1958. Today only one-eighth of the population are farmers. The decrease in percentage of farm population comes from an increase in urban population and an actual decrease in the number of farm workers resulting from improved methods and techniques on the farms. Farmers are using much more machinery (tractors, combines, cornpickers, cottonpickers, and milking machines, for example). There are "assembly-line" methods in use on large "integrated" poultry farms.

The second shift has been from the cities to the suburbs. The third notable shift has been from the agricultural states in the center of the country, particularly those in the Great Plains (some of which had decreases in population in the 1940's) to states on the west and east coasts. California, Oregon, Washington, Florida, Maryland, and Connecticut have had notable gains in population. A fourth shift has been that of Negroes from the Southeast to the industrial cities in the East and Mid-West. This migration became important in World War I and continued into the 1920's. The movement slowed up in the 1930's and increased greatly in the 1940's and 1950's. It is said to be one of the great migrations in history. Many of these Negroes are from rural areas and unused to life in large cities. They were no longer needed on farms because of the decline in cotton production and increased mechanization of agriculture. They moved north, attracted by higher wages. If one may judge by their facial expressions, they are less happy in the cities than they were on the farms and in the small towns.

All shifts in population are of interest to sellers, as they need to know where consumers are located.

Income

Income is one of the most important factors in determining markets. Disposable personal income (income after taxes) increased from $76 billion in 1940 to $151 billion in 1945, to $235 billion in 1952, to $287 billion in 1955. Allowing for increases in the consumer price index and population, this was an increase in "real" per capita income of 33 percent from 1940 to 1945, and an increase of 1 percent from 1945 to 1952, but 8 percent from 1944 to 1956. Allowing for the number of young children in the population in 1956, there was probably a noticeable increase in adult purchasing power over 1945. Per capita disposable income increased rapidly during World War II and slowly after 1945 (4 percent from 1945 to 1954). Not only was income high but consumers had large savings at the end of the war. During the 1940's there was a great leveling off of consumers' disposable incomes. This was due primarily to the highly graduated income taxes and to increased wages, overtime pay, and high employment. For example, in one industrial town in the mid-1940's, unskilled factory workers were paid seventy cents an hour—forty hours of work gave $28 a week earnings. But with twenty hours of overtime at $1.05, earnings were $49. Owing to the shortage of workers, men were quickly advanced and classified as skilled workers at $1.40 an hour or $56 a week. With twenty hours of overtime at $2.10 an hour, weekly earnings were $98 a week. There was somewhat higher pay for workers on the "graveyard" shift and on Sundays. Fifty weeks of work meant an income of $4,900 a year, and if there were two workers in a family, $9,800.

In 1956 the average wage of factory workers was around $2.00 per hour. If a man worked forty hours a week, had no overtime and no layoffs and missed no days, he would work two thousand hours a year for $4,000. There is an average of one and one-third workers per family, so the average factory worker family wage would be $5,333 if there were no layoffs and no overtime. An average may be important statistically; however, there are very few average families. A man on a job paying $1.37½ an hour with only one worker in the family, and the man having no second job, the family income would be $2,750. On the other hand, a family with two skilled workers rated at $2.75 per hour, neither having a second part-time job, would have an income of $11,000. Layoffs and overtime would decrease or increase these figures. Both families are factory workers, but the second has four times the income of the first.

Employers have found it hard to keep executives and trained technicians in line with other workers since in the higher salary brackets a larger percentage is taken by the tax collector. Various devices are used, such as stock options, annuities, and liberal expense allowances.

The following table shows the distribution of families in the various income groups in 1929, 1949, and 1958, based on the standard of living indicated by the income. The figures for 1929 and 1949 are averages of various estimates of income distribution.

TABLE 1

*Distribution of Families by Income
1929, 1949, and 1958*

Standard (scale) of living	Percentages of families		
	1929	1949	1958
Poverty	9.5	8	9.0
Bare subsistence	10.0	4	3.0
Minimum for health and efficiency	22.7	18	11.5
Minimum comfort	23.5	31	21.5
Comfort	15.6	20	31.0
Moderately well-to-do	10.5	15	14.0
Well-to-do	6.0	3	7.0
Liberal	2.2	1	3.0

As previously mentioned there was no leveling off during the 1930's. The graduated income tax was the main factor in the leveling off of family incomes (income which could be spent).

During World War II family incomes increased while the advance in the cost of living was limited. This helped particularly the lower income families who were little affected by the graduated income taxes. Family incomes increased as a result of full employment; an increase in the number of persons per family employed ("women welders," for example); payments for overtime; and in many instances a rapid upgrading of workers from unskilled to semiskilled, and to skilled. During the late 1940's there was a large demand for goods and for workers; and in many instances wages advanced faster than the cost of living.

In 1958 the proportion of families in the two lowest income groups was the same as in 1949. During the 1950's there was a considerable movement from the lower middle groups (minimum for

TABLE 2

The Leveling Off of Family Incomes, 1929–1958

	1929†		1958‡	
Standard* (scale) of living	Income needed to maintain standard	Percent of families	Income needed to maintain standard	Percent of families
Poverty	Under $750	9.5	Under $1,265	9.0
Bare subsistence	$ 750– 999	10.0	$ 1,266– 1,700	3.0
Minimum for health and efficiency	1,000–1,699	22.7	1,701– 2,870	11.5
Minimum comfort	1,700–2,599	23.5	2,871– 4,770	21.5
Comfort	2,600–3,999	15.6	4,771– 7,780	31.0
Moderately well-to-do	4,000–5,999	10.5	7,781–11,875	14.0
Well-to-do	6,000–9,999	6.0	11,876–19,600	7.0
Liberal	10,000 and over	2.2	Over 19,600	3.0
		100.0		100.0

* After Nystrom.
† Based on estimates of Nystrom and Brookings Institution.
‡ Figures rounded. Distribution based on estimates of the U. S. Department of Commerce (*Survey of Current Business,* April 1959) for a family of four dependents (man, wife, and 2 minor children) filing joint return (average size of family was 3.65 in 1957) and with 10 percent deductions for taxes, interest, charities, religion, and so on. No allowance is made for state income or other taxes aside from the federal income tax. The graduation in this tax partially explains the increase needed to maintain the higher standards.

Incomes of unattached individuals (outside family groups) are lower, presumably caused by the fact that a number of them are younger people who have not reached maximum earnings. (Also in this group would come many of the ne'er-do-wells and "work-shy" individuals.) Two-thirds of individuals are estimated by the Department of Commerce to have incomes under $5,000 and one-third under $3,000. The incomes of upper-income families come in considerable part from having two or more members employed.

health and efficiency, and minimum comfort) to the comfort group. There was also a very significant increase in the proportion of families in the two upper groups (well-to-do, and liberal). It appears that during this period the cost of living pretty well caught up with the increase in wages. However, salaries and bonuses of executives and the earnings of business and professional men more than made up for the graduation in income tax rates. It appears that the two upper income groups regained the relative position lost during the 1940's and that a larger proportion of families were in these groups than were in 1929. The estimates of number of families in the two upper income groups are apparently more accurate for 1958 than for 1929 and 1949.

Income Classes

It has been said that the United States is a classless society. This is largely, or partially, true if the statement is interpreted to mean a middle income or "middle class" society. It may be considered that the poverty and bare-subsistence groups make up the lower income (poor) class; the bare subsistence and minimum health-and-efficiency and minimum comfort groups, the lower middle income class; the comfort and moderately well-to-do groups, the upper middle class; and the well-to-do and liberal groups as the upper (prosperous) class. Under this grouping, one-eighth of the families are in the low income group; one-third in the lower middle class; somewhat less than one-half (45 percent) in the upper middle class; and one-tenth in the upper income class or group. Thus three-fourths of the families are in the middle class (income group.)*

The amount of income to maintain a given standard or scale of

* One concept is that the things that go to make up a given standard or scale of living change with time. This means that over long periods of time we should redefine the standards. When this is done, statistical comparisons are difficult.

The laborer of today, for example, has physical comforts not possessed by princes in ancient and mediaeval times. He has a better heated house, a better lighted house (window glass and electric lights), less annoyance from insects, better sanitation, better health protection, and faster and more comfortable transportation.

living varies with many factors, especially the number of members in the family and the place of residence. In many rural areas and small towns the cost of living and incomes are lower. In such places, a money income of $2,500 may enable a family to live as well or better than most of the families in the area and thus place it in the middle or upper class. On the other hand, the same income in a large city may only enable the family to live at the bare subsistence level.*

Purchase of Gadgets

There was a pent up demand for many types of goods. For some years there were not enough automobiles and household appliances to go around. The consumers bought and rented new homes as fast as they could be built. Many had to buy homes as the proportion of rental units tended to decline. Wartime rent controls were retained in some areas and limited the number of rental units built. The owners of some rental units found it more profitable to sell than to rent.

The consumers bought automobiles, furniture, radios, TV sets, aerials, home freezers, refrigerators, airplanes, food mixers, mangles, washing machines, clothes driers, electric garbage disposal units, dishwashers, vacuum cleaners, electric hair driers, water heaters, home heaters, electric stoves, lawn and garden equipment, stamps, picnic supplies, sporting goods, boats, skin diving equipment, movie cameras, still cameras, 3-D cameras, film, projectors, screens, toys, power tools, electric razors, silverware, watches, kitchen cabinets, carpets, domestic air conditioners, and dehumidifiers.

After the postwar pent up demand for automobiles, houses, furniture, and household appliances was filled, TV sets and home air conditioners became big sellers. The developments of suburbs brought about more outdoor living and demand for lawn furniture, sporting goods, garden and lawn tools and supplies, sport or informal clothes, ranch-type houses, and school buildings and equipment. Big new suburban housing developments were built on farm

* Someone defined an average as "a device for concealing the truth."

83

land and school boards called upon to supply schools where no schools had been needed. Rural electric lines increased the market for electric appliances, tools, and motors.

Highways deteriorated during the war. They had to be repaired and this took several years. New highways are being built to accommodate the new cars. Highways near large cities are badly congested. One almost wonders if the automobile will not defeat itself because there will be so many that the difficulty of driving and parking will decrease their use. Undoubtedly, parking difficulties have contributed to the sale of small cars, many of them imported.*

A partial solution is the building of toll roads and freeways. The Pennsylvania Turnpike, through the mountains from the Cumberland Valley to near Pittsburgh, proved a quick financial success and was followed by others. It was found that people would pay for use of a highway permitting somewhat higher speeds and having no stops. New Jersey, Connecticut, New York, Ohio, Massachusetts, New Hampshire, Maine, Indiana, Illinois, Oklahoma, Texas, and Kansas followed suit. The construction of these highways is expensive, many of them costing more than $1 million a mile. In comparison, the railroads are capitalized at $70 thousand a mile and this includes their locomotives, cars, freight yards, and other terminal facilities. Americans surely love their automobiles. The building of toll roads has just about stopped. They are now being replaced by the federal system of interstate freeways.

Capital Expenditures

Billions of dollars went into replacing and building new factories and buying new machinery. Railroads improved their roads and bought new diesel locomotives. New electric power plants were built and new transmission lines erected. Many new oil and gas wells were drilled, pipe lines and refineries built. Large deposits of oil and gas were found in Alberta and pipe lines built to Vancouver, Seattle, Duluth, and to eastern Canada. Large pipe lines

* "Conspicuous consumption" has also been a factor in the purchase of foreign cars.

(including the "Big Inch") were laid from Texas to the North Atlantic Coast during the war to move oil that except for German submarines would have been moved by tankers. Natural gas was taken from Texas to Boston and Los Angeles. New schools were built by the thousands. Atomic power passed from the pilot plant stage with the construction of commercial plants.

Research

Research increased rapidly. Many large industrial companies have hundreds and some have thousands of workers in their technical research departments. Some companies have scores of workers in their commercial research departments. Hundreds of new and improved products are being developed. All kinds of plastics are going into all kinds of products from toothbrushes to pipe lines. Synthetic fibers such as nylon, orlon, and dacron were placed on the market and sold in large quantities. After the success of the sulfas and the early antibiotics, drug manufacturers stepped up their research, spending some 5 percent of their receipts on research. So many new drugs have been placed on the market that 52 percent of the most frequently prescribed pharmaceutical specialties in 1954 were not on the market in 1949.

Atomic power passed through the pilot-plant stage with the construction of commercial atomic power plants.

Commercial research also increased rapidly. One pioneer researcher* says that in the 1900's and 1910's a business concern would spend from $10 to $100 for a research project while today some large companies are said to spend more than $1 million annually in business research. As late as 1944 a friend told me that there was not a single practicing market research man in one city of a million people. Today this city has a chapter of the American Marketing Association. Market research practitioners are now found in many towns of less than 100,000 population.

In the early 1930's it was guessed that American business was spending $100 million on research, of which 4 percent or $4 million went for marketing research. By the middle 1940's, it was guessed

* J. George Frederick.

that the total research bill was at over $2 billion, of which $100 million was for commercial research. In 1954 the guesses of the total annual cost of research were as high as $9 billion, of which $400 million were for marketing research. Thus in twenty-five years the expenditures for research have increased ninety-fold and the expenditures for marketing research a hundred-fold.

Services

With rising incomes the consumers tend to spend more money on services. Services include such things as education, travel, beauty parlors, sports, commercial amusements and entertainment, medical and hospital services. An interesting development has been the increased patronage of hospitals. Older people can remember when people only went to hospitals for surgery or the most critical illnesses. Today it appears that many go for minor ills and some perhaps to rest. Doctors like to have their patients in hospitals; they are easier to see and instructions are more likely to be followed. More people have hospital insurance, and they seem anxious to collect something for their premiums. The increased expenditure for services was evident in the 1920's and has continued.

Recession and Korea

By the summer of 1949 supply was pretty well catching up with the demand for automobiles, machines, and household appliances. Unemployment had declined to a low of 440,000 in October 1944. Unemployment then gradually increased after the war to between one and two million. It had increased to four million in July 1949. There was much talk about a recession. In one survey of factory workers, it was found that they were much interested in the sequence in which they should be laid off if this became necessary. Should the married women be laid off first? Should the work be spread by reducing the number of hours worked per week? Employers were talking about the workers improving their diligence when they heard there were people asking for jobs. There was, of course, much more unemployment in some areas than in others, depending upon the industries involved. National income declined only 2 percent from the first to the third quarter of the year. Unemployment decreased slightly during the fall of 1949, but increased in the winter to more than four and a half million in February 1950.

The Korean incident started in June 1950. There was an increase in the demand for munitions and an increase in the number of men in military service. Unemployment decreased considerably during the following months. No one knew how serious or how long continued the fighting would be. The government imposed some price controls. There was a rush to buy. Some bought in the fear that needed goods would again be scarce, and some for pure speculation. Prices increased almost 9 percent from September 1950 to February 1951.

It turned out that the fear of shortages was not well founded. Most of the shortages that did occur were the result of building up inventories or pure speculative buying. By the late spring of 1951, goods were again plentiful and wholesalers and retailers were curtailing their purchases until they worked their inventories down. Some of the speculative buyers had large losses.

Inflationary Hypothesis

Some persons are advancing the idea that the economic balloon must be continually inflated to keep businessmen and consumers optimistic so that they will continue to enlarge their plants, build more highways, and buy more goods to keep labor employed and to increase the national income so that more taxes can be collected. Periods of inflation ("booms") are periods of optimism and speculation. The idea is that optimism is necessary to keep the economy expanding. Since the output per worker increases some 2 percent a year, it is argued that prices and wages should advance 2 percent a year to enable the workers to buy the increased quantity of goods they produce.

There is something wrong with this argument; for if prices and wages are advanced as fast as production, the workers can buy only the same amount of goods as they did before. It would appear that prices should be reduced, so that the same income would buy more goods. Even if wages are advanced faster than prices, all the goods could not be sold to the consumers because only a part of the consumers are "wage earners." Only about one-half of the gainfully employed persons are laborers in the commonly accepted meaning of the word.* Salaried workers and people living from pensions, annuities, and interest have less purchasing power in periods of rising prices.

One wonders if the idea of keeping the inflationary spiral rising is not merely an attempt to postpone a "break" as long as possible. If the country wants to avoid depressions, the best way apparently is to keep prices flexible so that they keep demand in balance with supply.

Americans should develop more spiritual, moral, and cultural values and depend less on gadgets for happiness. Rich people are not the happiest people. Those who get the most satisfaction out of living are not those with the most gadgets and the most clothes. Basic in this civilization and religious culture is the philosophy that there are higher values than those based on gadgets, clothes, and gems. Just suppose that some day Russia catches up with the United States in material goods (physical standard of living)—will the United States be defeated? Not if this country has more important spiritual and mental values.

---

* Professional and technical workers, government employees, farmers, salesmen, managers, proprietors, officials, clerical workers, and military personnel make up more than one-half of the employed persons. Even if military personnel and clerical workers are omitted, still one-third of the workers are in the "fixed income" class—that is, workers whose income does not respond quickly to changes in wage rates. People living from pensions, annuities, interest, or rental of property covered by long-term leases have their purchasing power reduced by increased prices and can buy fewer goods and services. The incomes of people on salaries (managers, white collar workers, teachers, government employees, etc.) usually lag behind prices when prices rise, and hence they can buy fewer goods.

A recent research study of the American Federation of Labor and the Congress of Industrial Organizations (AFL-CIO) found that when all fringe benefits were considered, the pay of unionized laborers had fallen slightly behind the increased output per man hour. See *Labor, Big Business, and Inflation,* September 1958.

Free Trade and World Aid

The United States adopted high tariffs on many imported goods early in the nineteenth century. Producers said that they needed protection against the importation of foreign goods until they got their businesses established—the infant industry argument. It was said that a country should produce the goods necessary to defend itself in case of war and hence should develop factories making guns, ammunition, ships, and iron—the national defense argument. Others argued that import tariffs were desirable as they helped to develop manufacturing and so gave employment to more people and also enabled employers to pay higher wages. Farmers wanted tariffs on such products as wool and sugar which were imported to make the production of these products more profitable.

A producer would like to have a high import tariff on his product when some of it is imported as this would raise its price. He would like to have other goods imported without tariffs or with low tariffs as this would enable him to buy his raw materials at lower prices, would reduce the cost of living, and might enable him to employ workers at lower wages. However, no one producer has had enough political influence to secure such an arrangement. Therefore, those wanting high tariffs had to make common cause: *A* would support a high tariff on *B*'s product, and so in return *B* would support a high tariff on *A*'s product, and so on for all the others who wanted a high tariff. Thus, a protective tariff became a "cause," a "principle," and at times almost a "religion." Labor was largely won over on the argument that high tariffs make higher wages possible.

High tariffs can raise the price only when a product is imported or when domestic production is monopolized. When goods are exported, they must be sold at the price outside the United States, and the domestic price is not raised by the tariff—at least, it is not unless there is a monopoly which can sell at two prices. When a company comes to be an important importer, it is likely to change its ideas about a tariff. High tariffs in other countries give their producers an advantage and make it harder to sell goods to them. High tariffs in this country often lead other countries to retaliate and raise their tariffs on this country's goods. Thus, manufacturers interested in exporting usually favor low tariffs. If nations are to buy goods from the United States, they must be able to pay for them in goods or with money obtained from exporting goods to other countries. They must have industries capable of producing goods at costs enabling them to sell abroad.

There has been quite a change in feelings about tariffs in the United States during the past thirty years as the importance of its export trade has increased. Many businesses in the United States have become export or world trade conscious. This has been reflected in governmental action in lowering tariffs and in the negotiation of reciprocity treaties with other countries leading to mutually lower tariffs.

The United States helped to rebuild Europe and particularly Germany after World War I. The program of aid to foreign countries has been greatly expanded since World War II and has amounted to around $100 billion. A considerable part of this aid has been for military purposes, but much of it has been for strengthening the economies of friendly countries so that they could buy American goods. In other words, the American government loans or gives money to various countries so that they can buy goods in the United States. Insofar as the loans are made to good credit risks who will repay them, this looks like good business. If the loans are not repaid or if outright gifts are made, the United States is in effect giving goods away to maintain its own economy and prevent unemployment. This is a new kind of economics; in short, the United States is giving goods away so that it can have the fun of making them.

Foreign aid has taken other forms, including expert advice by specialists, loan of teachers, and bringing foreign students, businessmen, and workmen here to study American methods. The output per worker in American factories and on American farms is higher than in most other countries. Businessmen, engineers, workers, and students are brought here to study, observe, and learn methods so that they can go home and improve their methods of production and distribution.

This is a new and rather strange procedure in this old world. In the past, when a country got an advantage, it tried to keep it. If it had better machines, it tried to prevent their export and the export of plans and specifications from which they could be made. The same has been applied to better breeds of animals, or to better techniques of production. But the United States is saying to the world: "Come look over our plants, our methods, our life, and learn all you can from us, and then go home and increase your own productive efficiency, your economy, and the scale of living of your people so that you will be able to buy more of our goods." It is hoped that they will not only have a more prosperous economy but will also be friends to the United States. They may also be tougher competitors. However, it is felt that the American free enterprise and educational systems will enable the United States to keep the lead; or at least not to be outdistanced in the competitive struggle.

There are some skeptics who are wondering if the United States is not too generous and that these people will use their increased knowledge and efficiency to outdistance the United States in business and to fight America as the Germans used the help which was given them in the 1920's and the 1930's to fight the United States in the 1940's.

Suburban Shopping Centers

One of the most notable developments in the decade following World War II was the growth of the suburban shopping center. As was previously noted, suburban business districts had been growing and downtown department stores had been opening branch stores in the suburbs. The planned shopping center is different. Usually a sizable tract of land is purchased upon which are placed several stores and a large parking lot. Often the land was unoccupied or only partially built up and near a suburb.

Shopping centers vary from a few acres having a supermarket and a few other stores to those having fifty to a hundred acres with department stores, clothing stores, dress shops, shoe stores, variety stores, drug stores, beauty parlors, restaurants, picture theaters, filling stations, and other types of business and service. It is now felt that such large centers should have two department stores. Some are so large that it is a considerable distance from parked cars to stores. Present practice is to devote three-fourths to four-fifths of the space to parking. It is debated whether a supermarket should locate in such centers, as these centers are primarily for shopping goods. If a supermarket is located there, it should be at the opposite end from the department stores. Shoppers can drive from one end to the other and park if they buy both clothing and food. Women will visit the food store in slacks, or housedresses, without primping. But when they visit the apparel and department stores, they like to be better dressed.

The shopping centers are well adapted to customers with automobiles. Drivers will go several blocks farther to patronize a store with ample parking space in preference to a closer store with no parking space.

Undoubtedly, some mistakes have been and will be made in developing shopping centers. Once built, a shopping center will be there for years. It cannot be moved. These centers have set a pattern that will be used for many years.

Offices in the Suburbs

One should mention in passing the "flight to the suburbs" of offices. One advantage of suburban locations is their greater convenience to the workers. Many of them can walk to work or can drive and park their cars in company parking lots. This helps morale. There are, on the other hand, several disadvantages of locating offices in the suburbs, including distance from customers and various service industries. The disadvantages seem to be of sufficient importance to slow or to check the movement to the suburbs. In the late 1950's new office buildings have been and are being built in the central areas of cities. A few downtown department stores have converted unneeded space into offices, and more may do so.

Downtown business and retail districts will continue to be important. However, the loss of business to the suburbs has been so great that businesses in many downtown locations have organized for cooperative action to hold their own. Real estate values and taxes may be reduced in central business districts. In retailing, the larger stocks and greater assortments of goods in the larger downtown stores will apparently hold much trade. Office organizations that need to be near customers, banks, brokers, a variety of skilled workers, supply houses, railway terminals, hotels, or service industries will likely remain in downtown locations. If it were not for such convenience, there would not have been the growth of large cities.

Movement of Factories to the Country

Industries are decentralizing and placing new plants in different towns and in different parts of the country. There has been considerable industrialization on the West Coast, particularly to supply growing local markets. There has been much development in the Central West and Middle South. One reason given for this decentralization is the fear of bombing of the larger cities in case of war. This may be a sound reason. However, this gives little assurance of continued production in case of bombings unless there is regional integration. It gives little protection to make some parts and assemble the completed machine south of the Ohio River if essential parts must be brought from Ohio or Michigan. To get assured production, all parts made from the basic steel and plastics must be produced in different parts of the country.

Plants are decentralized to get closer to markets, to get closer to raw materials, and to locate where labor is available, or where wages are lower. It was formerly said (prior to 1930) that when skilled labor was needed to operate a plant, it was desirable to locate in areas where skilled labor was plentiful. This does not seem to be nearly as important as formerly. Americans as a whole are machine minded and have a great deal more mechanical know-how than was the case a generation ago. More machines are automatic or semiautomatic and can use unskilled or semiskilled labor. It has been found in a great many instances that a factory can start with unskilled labor and a few instructors and in a very short time turn out products that pass rigid quality tests.

It is said that plants now often locate in agricultural areas not so much for low wages and absence of labor unions as to obtain new workers who can be trained to work as the companies want them to work. The new workers do not have to unlearn anything. They have no fixed ideas as to stints or quotas nor as to work habits and procedures.

Increase in Self-Service

Supermarkets have continued to grow and to add additional lines of goods to their stocks. Self-service or super drugstores were started on the West Coast some years ago. They gradually spread and a few were started in the Middle West before World War II. They have been growing rather rapidly since 1945. If the supermarket sells drugs and toilet articles, the self-service drugstore may be a good way for the druggist to meet the competition. More price competition may be expected between the supermarkets and the super drugstores.

Many other types of stores are using the self-service and self-help methods in some or all their lines of goods.

Discount Selling

Another spectacular development of the 1950's is the discount selling. The discount house is a leader in this. It sells household appliances and many other types of merchandise to the consumer at reduced or "wholesale" prices. The discount house apparently had its principal origin in the buying club. The members of buying clubs received discounts when they patronized certain stores. At times, all or most of the stores in a retail district offered discounts to buying club members. In other cases, the buying club directed its members to the named cooperating stores. Often membership cards could be had for the asking. Another root was the dealers who sold "wholesale."

Discount houses operate in many ways. Some sell by mail. Many carry goods on the floor for immediate delivery. Some charge membership dues. Some sell only to those having membership cards. A separate charge may be made for delivery and installation or the house or the manufacturer may make delivery and installation free when this is necessary. Discount houses feature nationally known brands. They may buy from the manufacturer, his distributors, or dealers. They may buy job lots. They often undersell retailers by as much as 10 percent to 35 percent. Estimates of their sales varied from $10 billion to $25 billion in 1954. Of the business in the lines they handle, $10 billion represents a very sizable "chunk."

It is often asked how they can sell so much lower than the orthodox retailers. Various reasons are given. They operate on a limited service basis. They may be located outside the high rent district, perhaps in warehouses or on upper floors. Many do little advertising and use little salesmanship. In fact, many of the buyers are "presold." This is perhaps the key to their growth. An article often changes its classification with time. A new article may be a "specialty" that must be actively promoted. The consumers are skeptical. Perhaps demonstrations are needed. Washing machines were formerly taken to the homes of prospects and their operation demonstrated by the salesmen. The goods had to be explained to the consumers. Consumers wanted to think over the purchase and often had to be persuaded to buy or to take the goods on approval. As the product wins acceptance, less salesmanship and promotion are needed. Retailers are able to handle the product on lower margins. These facts are often overlooked by manufacturers.

Products requiring active promotion at one time may later be adapted to the supermarket type of selling, in which the consumer picks out the goods and pays cash for them. If credit is needed, it is supplied by a bank or a finance company. Many household appliances, home furnishings, silverware, clocks, kitchen equipment, radios, and TV sets can be sold in this way. If the manufacturer "sells" his goods to the consumers, why does the retailer have to "sell" them again? The retailer in this case acts largely as a physical distributor of the goods. The mail-order chains have been operating more or less in this way for some years.

It has been said that every new market institution (chain store, mail-order house, supermarket, discount house, for example) enters the market on the basis of price, but that over time it loses much or all of its price advantage. This may come from competitors increasing their operating efficiency or adopting the methods used by the newcomer, or from the newcomer losing much of its operating efficiency or introducing more services.

Department stores are using warehouse sales while other established retailers are introducing discount-house methods. Discount houses are increasing their services (credit, for example), and carrying wider stocks.

Physical Handling

Less known to the public but perhaps more important than the discount house has been the increase in the mechanical handling of goods. The change in physical handling since 1940 has been revolutionary. Many mechanical devices are used but the more important ones are fork-lift trucks, pallets, and one-story warehouses. The pallet is a platform, usually made of rough lumber and perhaps 40 x 48 inches. Goods are stacked on this and moved from place to place and stacked by the fork-lift truck which is operated by either a storage battery or a gasoline engine. The one-story warehouse saves the time and cost of moving goods up and down as is necessary in a multistory warehouse. The combination—one-story warehouses, fork-lift trucks, and pallets reduce the amount of labor required in handling goods by some 25 percent. This method of handling goods came into some use in the 1920's, but it has been since 1940, and especially since 1945, that its use has been widespread. The one-story warehouse often means a move from the congested downtown sections to the suburbs where land is cheaper and streets less congested so that trucks can move faster. The multistory warehouses exist and will be in use for years. As the demand for space in them declines, the rent may decrease so that there is less difference in the cost of operation between them and the newer one-story warehouses.

Diversification and Mixed Lines

An important development in the 1940's that has gained momentum in the 1950's has been that of diversifying lines. As one manufacturer put it: "Everyone is trying to get into everyone else's business." A farm implement manufacturer makes trucks and refrigerators; an automobile manufacturer makes air conditioning equipment. One company makes chemicals, drugs, toilet articles, cigarette paper, rocket engines, ammunition, firearms, cellophane, brass, and plastics. This company has some fifteen hundred people in its research departments. Another company makes radar sets, radios, TV's, stoves, and air cleaners. These are all concerned with electronics but are sold through different trade channels. Many retailers are widening their lines; notable are the supermarkets, but drug, hardware, and department stores are not far behind.

In the past it has been thought that there were many sound advantages to specialization and that wastes were involved in handling a variety of products. In the 1920's much was heard of simplification, and its advantages were widely extolled. Then why the change to the other extreme?

There may be several reasons. There is the natural desire for growth, and one way to increase sales is to add more products. New products come into use and old ones go out of use or decrease in sales in relatively short periods. Thus the adding of new products is regarded as insurance of continued sales in the future. Large research organizations make possible the development of new products and the ascertaining of which products have sales possibilities. World War II and the postwar boom gave many companies the capital needed for expansion. The consumers have money and new products may sell readily.

Nevertheless, one wonders if all this diversification is sound, especially when the products reach different markets through different trade channels. Is there not a danger of spreading management too thin? Efficiency can often be increased through specialization.

Theory of the Gadget Economy, the 1950's

The widely held theory of business in the 1950's is that there should be more salesmanship, more advertising, more display of goods, more publicity, more point-of-sale promotion—to sell more goods, to prevent unemployment. In short, it is felt that a lot of high-pressure selling is needed to induce the consumers to buy enough goods to keep the economic system operating at high speed and to prevent unemployment. Unemployment is thought of as the worst catastrophe that can happen. Therefore, consumers must buy more gadgets whether or not they need them to keep the economic system functioning and to keep men at work.

If new gadgets cannot be found that the consumers will buy, then the same gadgets should be made in different colors, or styles, and so make the present gadgets obsolete, to make the consumers dissatisfied with what they have so they will spend for something that seems to be different. Put shelves on the doors of refrigerators; put more cylinders in the motor; put more horsepower under the hood; put high ovens on stoves so cooks do not have to stoop over to reach them, and when the market is saturated with stoves with high ovens, make stoves with low ovens and griddles on top. Then have detached "built-in ovens." Keep the consumer dissatisfied by the feeling that the newer gadgets are "better" or more fashionable. This has been called "progressive obsolescence."

The theory of gadgets has gone so far that some manufacturers feel that a large part of their sales in 1970 will be made up of gadgets not yet perfected. To assure the future of a company means that more and better research men are necessary to invent, develop, perfect, and test the new gadgets. If the consumers will not accept one gadget, another must be found. Thus consumer research may be as important as laboratory research and workshop skill.

If the gadgets are useful and needed, this sounds like a good philosophy. If, on the other hand, the gadgets are of little value to the consumers, it would appear that the work of producing and selling them is wasteful.

Why all the fear of unemployment? Throughout history, work has been considered unpleasant and irksome. When Adam and Eve were thrown out of the Garden of Eden for sinning, a large part of their punishment was that they had to go to work to earn their bread. The Christian's concept of heaven down through the ages has been a place where there was no work. Why all this turn about? Why is unemployment such a catastrophe?

The reason is that for urban workers no work means no income (except unemployment pay or a relief dole). Therefore, unemployment means hardship, or at least a drop in the scale of living. However, if the country has all the goods it needs, it seems foolish to make more goods, just to keep busy. Some other way should be found out of the dilemma.

There are other angles to this story. It assumes that many people, probably most people, need many more gadgets than they now have. To have more goods would make them happier and enable them to get more satisfaction out of life, or so runs the argument. To the extent that this is true, the theory has a desirable goal.

The common opinion is that the more gadgets one has the happier he is. If one has a gas stove, he is happier than if he has to cook on a coal stove. If he has a bathtub, he is happier than if he has to bathe in a washtub. If one has a horse, he is happier than if he has to walk. If he has an auto, he is happier than if he has to use a horse. If one has an automobile with six cylinders, he is happier than with one that has only four cylinders. If one has an automobile with a 200-horsepower motor, he is twice as happy as with only a 100-horsepower motor. If one has a phonograph, he is happier than if he has a piano. If he has a radio, he is happier than with a phonograph. If one has TV, he is happier than with a radio. If one has electric lights, he is happier than if he has kerosene lamps; and if one has a camera using colored film, he is happier than with one that uses black and white film. And so *ad infinitum*.

Since the majority of American families have many of these things, then the American family should be many times happier than it was in 1900. Such is not the case. There are more people in mental institutions. There seem to be more suicides, more psychiatrists, more nervous breakdowns, and more columns giving advice and solace to the disappointed.

Obviously, more gadgets will not give one happiness, satisfaction, tranquillity, and a fuller life. These must come from within, from spiritual resources. Pleasures and happiness cannot be measured by the price tags on gadgets. The little things, the simple things, may be the most important ones. One should get satisfaction out of the little things in his daily life, out of work, out of associations and friendships with fellow workers and neighbors.

Another angle is the ability to increase total sales by more salesmanship. It was formerly the common opinion among economists that there was only a certain amount of purchasing power, and that if one seller cried his goods louder and sold more, the sales of other sellers would decline. It is now realized by many economists that people have the ability to increase their incomes and that they will do so given the opportunity. To produce more goods, people had to be employed and expenditures made for labor, materials, equipment, power, and the like. The people receiving these payments have the money with which to make purchases. The producing of one product enables the workers to buy other goods. The businessman (entrepreneur) who makes new things, or who makes more of already accepted goods, is the man primarily responsible for economic progress. Next is the research man who develops new products, who finds markets for new products, or finds how products should be improved to better serve the consumers. The whole operation would be useless unless the salesmen and the advertising men could go out and tell the consumers about the goods.

The business would fail unless the consumers bought the goods. (The gadgeteers largely overlook the increase in demand possible through lower prices.) The consumers cannot buy the goods unless they secure the necessary purchasing power through their own efforts. Business is a cycle. Goods cannot be produced unless there is a demand for them. There can be no demand unless goods are produced to create the demand. This is a fine system when it works. It has raised the scale of living and can raise it higher. But it is a sensitive system and one that easily gets out of balance. It has usually gotten out of balance once in every generation. Present thinking is that government controls and regulations can keep the machine oiled and operating without breakdowns. But government is made up of people. People have limited information, imagination, and outlook.* A better view is that government may postpone a breakdown, but the postponement may mean that the break will be worse when the wreck comes.

To think is to wonder where one is going. Machinery is constantly being improved. New automatic machines are being introduced which make things with less and less labor. (The labor in building the machines, which is considerable, must not be overlooked.) One stops in wonderment when he reads of the possibilities for atomic power. Are there soon to be more goods than there is time to use? Already being invented are new sports, hobbies, and recreation activities to occupy leisure time. Unemployed youth gets into much

* The decade of the 1930's shows the limitations in the minds of individuals. President Hoover could not bring himself to declare a banking moratorium and restore confidence in the banks. President Roosevelt did this but then almost immediately launched the NRA which definitely retarded recovery.

mischief; perhaps the schools should give much more homework and perhaps the age for employment should be reduced. Must more and more things be consumed just to keep people busy making them? Leisure is often less interesting than work. Is work going to become "play" and "play" become "work" so that people can have the fun of making the gadgets consumed in "leisure" time? Or is the fine art of loafing to be redeveloped?

People are told that progress ceases when they stop working. Progress can be made only by striving and working, so runs the argument. People must be made to work if they are to grow and develop either mentally or physically. An unused cell does not develop. The incentive to work may be a slave driver's whip, or a reward attainable only through exertion. The reward should be something the individual wants. In the present-day United States, rewards consist of better food, clothing, houses, and gadgets of every and all descriptions. People weigh or balance the pleasure to be obtained from additional gadgets against the pleasure of leisure-time activities or just the pleasure of loafing. High-pressure salesmanship and advertising seem to make people feel that the gadgets are more worthwhile than leisure. This is true to the extent that millions of people have more than one job.[*]

On the other side of the picture is the fact that the world's population is increasing. That of the United States is increasing at a surprisingly rapid rate. If this rate of increase continues, it may itself check the increase in the scale of living. All raw materials must come from nature—the soil, minerals in the ground, or chemical substances in the atmosphere and the sea. Thus, there is a mathematical limit to the population that can be supported on the earth. If the tropics can be conquered and its millions of acres of fertile land put into cultivation, the world could support a considerably larger population at a higher scale of living than it now has. So far, this has not been done. It would be my guess that the people in the United States will again reduce the birth rate before they allow the scale of living to decrease substantially. This suggests that the birth rate may serve as a kind of balance wheel. If the desired scale of living cannot be maintained because of the large population (in

[*] People having two jobs are popularly referred to as "moonlighters."

relation to resources), people will have fewer children. Personal income will decline. Young people will postpone marriage. Older marriages mean fewer children per family. This slows up the rate of population growth and may continue until population declines. With the reduced population, incomes increase until the birth rate again rises. This is at least a plausible theory.

Conclusions

The work week has been shortened and employment has been high. More than sixty-five million people are employed. There are somewhat over forty million families plus perhaps five million or more individuals outside of families who are in the labor force. A great many families have two or three workers. Many of the second workers are wives. It has been estimated that twelve million married women are employed. There would seem to be many advantages in having the husband employed more hours per week, bringing prices down to where one worker could support the family, and in having the wives devote more of their time to homemaking and education and training of their children. The short work week tends to defeat itself. There are millions of people having two jobs, usually one full-time or regular job and one part-time or irregular job.

The wage scale is so high that many families cannot afford to hire needed repairs on their homes. There are a great many "do it yourself" campaigns. They cover painting, carpentry, plumbing, roofing, and many other jobs. This means that people doing their own repair and building jobs are doing work in which they are amateurs. It might be better for them to work longer hours in their vocations and hire skilled men to make repairs.

Perhaps the greatest fear today is that of unemployment. If a city worker loses his job and cannot find another, he is in a serious situation. Few can return to the land. Many are too old to enlist in military service. The unemployed worker has rent to pay and installments to meet on many of his unpaid-for gadgets. The fear of unemployment has led to demands for job security, seniority rights, unemployment compensation, and old age pensions. Young men looking for their first jobs often inquire about job security and retirement pay. Retirement plans often involve high deductions from pay checks. Throughout history, many people have been willing to sacrifice freedom for security. One must wonder if Americans are falling into this category. Many seem satisfied to trade individual liberty for security.

Regardless of the desire for security and the theories of economics and government this country is following, Americans are living in an age of gadgets. The more gadgets—the more happiness—or so runs the argument. Whether or not this is good for the soul and the mind, Americans go merrily gadgeting on their way. Where the way leads no one knows and no one seems to care.

A CENTURY OF MARKETING

An Arno Press Collection

Alderson, Wroe. **Marketing Behavior and Executive Action.** 1957
Assael, Henry, editor. **The Collected Works of C. C. Parlin.** 1978
Assael, Henry, editor. **Early Development and Conceptualization of the Field of Marketing.** 1978
Assael, Henry, editor. **A Pioneer in Marketing, L. D. H. Weld.** 1978
Bartels, Robert D. W. **Marketing Literature: Development and Appraisal.** 1978
Blankenship, Albert B. **Consumer and Opinion Research.** 1943
Borden, Neil H. **Advertising in Our Economy.** 1945
Breyer, Ralph F. **The Marketing Institution.** 1934
Breyer, Ralph F. **Quantitative Systemic Analysis and Control.** 1949
Clark, Fred E. **Principles of Marketing.** 1922
Clark, Lincoln H., editor. **Consumer Behavior.** 1958
Coles, Jessie V. **The Consumer-Buyer and the Market.** 1938
Collins, V[irgil] D[ewey]. **World Marketing.** 1935
Converse, Paul D. **The Beginning of Marketing Thought in the U.S.** *and* **Fifty Years of Marketing in Retrospect.** 1959
Copeland, Melvin Thomas. **Principles of Merchandising.** 1924
The Ethical Problems of Modern Advertising. 1931
Frederick, John H. **Industrial Marketing.** 1934
Frederick, J. George. **Modern Salesmanagement.** 1921
Hower, Ralph M. **The History of an Advertising Agency.** 1939
Longman, Donald R. **Distribution Cost Analysis.** 1941
Lyon, Leverett S. **Salesmen in Marketing Strategy.** 1926
The Men Who Advertise. 1870
Nystrom, Paul H. **Economics of Retailing.** 1930
Reilly, William J. **Marketing Investigations.** 1929
Revzan, David A. **Wholesaling in Marketing Organization.** 1961
Rosenberg, Larry J., editor. **The Roots of Marketing Strategy.** 1978
Scott, Walter Dill. **The Psychology of Advertising.** 1913
Sorenson, Helen. **The Consumer Movement.** 1941
Starch, Daniel. **Advertising Principles.** 1927
Terry, Samuel Hough. **The Retailer's Manual.** 1869
Tosdal, Harry R. **Principles of Personal Selling.** 1925
White, Percival. **Advertising Research.** 1927
White, Percival. **Scientific Marketing Management.** 1927

HF
5415.1
.C59
1978

HF
5415.1
.C59

1978